Celebrity
Regressions

Celebrity
Regressions

Lee Everett

foulsham

LONDON • NEW YORK • TORONTO • SYDNEY

foulsham

The Publishing House, Bennetts Close,
Cippenham, Berkshire SL1 5AP, England.

ISBN 0–572–02297–2

Typeset in Great Britain by Typesetting Solutions, Slough, Berkshire.
Printed in Great Britain by St. Edmundsbury Press, Bury St. Edmunds, Suffolk.

Contents

*I would like to dedicate this book
to all my helpers on the other side.*

❖

CHAPTER ONE

Introducing Regressional Therapy

Sister Teresa was shocked from her quiet thoughts as she tended her herb garden. She heard cries and shouts. There was some kind of disturbance in the convent grounds. Dropping her tools, she hurried off to find out what was happening, and to her utter horror discovered her world as she knew it being destroyed. The usually peaceful corridors reverberated with the terrified screams of her sisters. There were soldiers everywhere, slashing at and wrecking all before them. They were acting like monsters, raping and pillaging, obviously turned on by the terror, excited by the power of fear. Rough hands threw her against the cloister walls. Her nightmare began . . .

They were cramped and cold in their dark, dungeon prison. Some prayed, others whimpered, while others lay so deep in shock it was as if they were dead. Sister Teresa tried to stay calm, turning to God to pray for help for them all. She felt responsible. It was she who had spoken out so freely and passionately against the Inquisition; she who had shown no terror, only contempt, when the whole of Spain reeked with the stench of fear. In her heart she knew the price she would have to pay for her beliefs; it was part of her path, her test of faith, all their tests of faith.

She was abruptly snapped out of her reveries by the sound of the huge metal doors being thrown back. As she looked into the man's eyes, she knew the time had arrived. He had come for her. She was singled out, for she was the Mother Superior, and for many years she had been like a mother to her girls. Rough hands pulled her to her feet and shoved her unceremoniously down the dark corridors until she was face to face with the man she knew would be her torturer.

He sat in front of a large, dark chest of drawers, his eyebrows so bushy they met in the middle. It was too difficult to look at him – she couldn't do it – so she tried to keep her eyes on the chest behind him. Now she must be strong; she must show the courage of her convictions; she must never renounce her faith.

The long days and nights of torture that followed seemed endless. How much longer could a human body suffer before some kind of release came? Constantly she prayed for death, she prayed for strength, she prayed for the sisters, and her prayers helped to fill her mind. But constantly she feared she would succumb. There was not a bone left unbroken in her body and the pain was relentless. At times she felt as though she had been totally forsaken, and only the feeling that she must be an example to her sisters kept her from going under, for she knew that if she broke, all would fall. Then, finally, the blessed relief of death. She no longer feared the flames for they gave her a longed-for release. She had made it; she had not betrayed her God. The awesome white light encased her, healing her and claiming her. She was home . . .

It had all seemed like a nightmare, but I had been wide awake the whole time. I had just been put into regression, where I had revisited an experience that had actually happened to me hundreds of years ago. I had just relived part of a past incarnation.

I was born believing in reincarnation. In fact, it wasn't until I was in junior school that I had realised I was fairly unusual in this belief. I had been chatting happily in the playground about past life and what I wanted to be in my next one, and it suddenly hit me that everyone thought I was joking! Not a single person there had even given any thought to such things. Later on, at home, I looked back on that incident and realised that I had no idea where this knowledge came from. It was certainly not from my parents or relatives; nothing of that nature had ever been discussed. It was then – at that early age – I realised that this was an inner knowledge I possessed, a thing that I somehow knew and was sure about.

From that time on I hardly ever mentioned my beliefs to my family or friends, as I felt they were rather like a religion, something that should not be argued over, since without proof the argument could go nowhere. My convictions were unshakeable, so why should I expect anyone else to go against their equally strongly held beliefs.

So you can imagine my joy at finding actual proof that my past lives really existed. I had already had proof of another aspect of this earlier in my life, but I'll deal with that later in the book.

I had never had any definite ideas of who or what I had been before this life, yet here I was presented with a nun who had come into my life a year ago and turned my whole world upside down.

It had happened in my mid-thirties. My life had been, to say the least, eventful. I was married to a well-known personality, the television performer Kenny Everett, who was often overcome by deep, black depressions which had reached the stage of being almost tangible they were so intense. I could see the black clouds that surrounded him; I would even find those clouds engulfing the entire house. I was desperate to find help for this man whom I loved. Despite all my prayers, things only became worse. Finally I had decided that my prayers were not strong enough, so I decided to offer them up in a church to try to give them more power. I chose a Spiritualist Church as that seemed closest to how I felt and what I believed in. I found that I had chosen the right route as it led not only to my husband's cure, but after that to a cure for the chronic asthma I had developed during my extremely eventful life.

We were living in the Cotswolds at that time and I discovered that the nearest Spiritualist Church was held in a hired hall every Sunday in Stratford-on-Avon. I wearily made my way there but had trouble locating the place and finally arrived after the service had started. I quietly took my place in the empty back row and sat down and tried to gather what was happening. There was a lady standing up on the platform speaking to various members of the congregation; I later realised that she was a visiting medium. She was giving messages of comfort to some of the people, but suddenly pointed at me and said she wished to speak to the lady at the back of the hall wearing a red coat. She told me that she was being told I had come to ask for help. I had to affirm this. She told me that she could see a cat at my window who was distressed at not being let in! (This was perfectly true as when my asthma had reached a very bad peak I could not live with the cat hairs so had had to make a home for my pet outside in an outhouse.) She then told me that she felt the answer to my plea for help would come from a sort of screen, but then realised that it was in fact a book that held the information. I was told that this would be brought forward very soon, then she moved on to another needy person. After the service I went home in a haze of thoughts and gratitude but felt that it was more like a miracle I needed, not a book! The first thing I did when I got home was let the cat back into the house; in fact she was there to greet me when I drove into the garage.

The next day I had to go and do some shopping and collect Ev's (my name for Kenny) regular prescription for sleeping pills. I would normally leave the prescription at the chemist and return after the shopping to collect it, but this particular day I was so exhausted and at the end of my tether that I flopped down in the chair provided and waited. I stared straight ahead and there – directly in my line of sight propped up by the till – I saw a booklet with wavy lines of the title written on it like snores, *Sleeping But Not Sleeping*. It was the British Medical Association's book on sleeping pills. As I paid for the pills I also purchased the book, dropped it in my bag and promptly forgot all about it. When I returned to our home, Ev was waiting in an agitated state and told me that one of our horses had collided with some barbed wire and had a severe cut on her rump. I deposited my bags in the kitchen and rushed into the fields to tend to our mare. I was out in the stables for about an hour and when I returned the miracle had happened. Ev had put all the shopping away whilst I was out and had come across the new booklet and read it straight through. He had a look of hope on his face and asked me to sit down whilst he read the whole text to me.

'It's a description of me, Lee,' he said. The newly acquired reading matter described the effects of taking sleeping pills over long periods, and the deep depressions that are the side effects. He really was a role model for the piece. He had been taking these awful pills long before I had met him so I had nothing to judge his moods against. From that day on he never took another one.

Coming off the pills was really terrible, however. He could not sleep so we both played cards most of the night until he fell asleep through sheer exhaustion. Then when he did finally drop off he would have horrific nightmares, rather like an alcoholic's pink elephants. One night he woke me with his shrill screams of fear, saying he had seen an old hag of a woman at the bottom of his bed with jagged teeth trying to eat his feet. It took weeks before he began to sleep properly unaided. I was quite literally ready to drop, but we stuck at it together and conquered his habit.

It really was a miracle because his whole mood changed to a jolly, bright and happy husband. Yes, my prayers had been answered. I thanked God every day for years after that. I also became very involved with the church and went on a private session to see the medium whose message had changed our lives. She told me to go away and do breathing exercises that she described to me and that I would be cured of my asthma.

This also came true; in fact I never had an attack from that day onwards. At the same sitting, she saw a bottle of alcohol and said that she saw someone who was helping me knock the bottle off the table. I knew what was meant by that as I had taken to drinking rather heavily and regularly to ease the pain of my life. I went home and gave up drinking for a couple of years to clean out my system.

This in its turn led me to discover that I had the gift of healing. After I had seen Ev become well, I became so dedicated to what I felt was spiritual help that I began sitting in a circle to expand my faith. On the very first weekly sitting of this group that I arranged to be held at my home, I first saw my nun, Sister Theresa. In fact, the first session we held showed us many wonderful signs.

My mother had died during the previous year and I had many of her possessions around the house in her memory. One of these was a chiming clock that did a sort of Big Ben imitation every quarter of an hour. I loved it as it reminded me of my very happy childhood, but the noise drove Ev mad so we had stopped winding it and it had stood mutely in the hall ever since. But on the evening that my new spiritual friends arrived, the clock chimed away madly the full stroke of twelve, then fell back to silence. I looked at it in amazement to find it was not even ticking! The second spooky thing that occurred was after the meditation when I opened the cupboard to offer my guests a drink. I found that my mother's hat had been placed on the bottles. I had sent all her clothes to the local hospital so you can imagine my surprise. Before she had died we had spent hours having drinks from this same cupboard and I had explained my beliefs about life after death many times, but she always said that when you died you dried up and blew away. But when she was dying she had vowed that if she found that death was not a final ending she would try and find a way to help me and repay me for all I had done for her in the ten years since my father had left her a widow. I guessed that the hat and clock was her way of telling me she now agreed with me, and I also felt she was showing her joy at the new path I had chosen, or was it already chosen for me?

After many months of this work I discovered that I had an extreme power building with me and was often aware of not being alone. I had purchased a tiny runt of a Chihuahua puppy that was minute but divine. I had owned a Chihuahua before called Bowbells – another tiny runt – and had missed her very much when she had died at the age of fifteen. I had always felt that she was irreplaceable. One day I was in a local bakery when a lady came in with the dead ringer for Bowbells. We naturally got talking and she told me that her pup had a sister that was for sale but was even tinier. Of course, I ended up purchasing her and I called her Totty. When my sister heard what I had named my new baby she reminded me that when Mam could not remember a girl's name she always called them Totty Ann, so I felt that my puppy had been sort of a gift from my mother. (Strangely enough years later, just after Ev died, I found myself in a position where I was again guided to my present Chihuahua which I felt was a gift from him.)

This tiny soul had certainly opened my heart as I slept with her and poured love on her. She had developed a bad habit of following us to the car and standing on her hind legs up to the edge of the door to be lifted in. I was always warning Ev to look before closing the door of his car and, predictably, one day he slammed the heavy car door on her tiny body and she fell into a coma and went stiff as a board. As we rushed her to the vet, I held her in my arms, devastated. The vet examined her and said that he would have to put her to sleep as even if she ever regained consciousness she would never be right again. I flatly refused to let this happen and returned home with her. Ev was distraught with guilt as he knew how much she meant to me. I decided that my only hope was to pray. I strapped her to my body with crepe bandages and went to bed with her. Finally, I fell into an exhausted sleep.

I woke early the next morning and unstrapped my little bundle to find that she jumped happily around the room as if nothing had happened. I wakened Ev and we both decided that yet another miracle had happened. I had been the channel for the healing of my Totty. That was not the end of the matter, though, as the next night I went to bed accompanied by my pet and lay with my hand on her body. Suddenly I felt a huge bubble grow under my hand and begin to move down her body under her skin. I pulled the covers back and held her up to witness this weird bubble reach her back passage and a mass of black matter shoot out with such force that it covered the wall opposite. It seemed to me that this was the clearance of her accident as she was never troubled again. I went on from there to be the healing channel not only for animals but for many people.

From the time of getting help for Ev, I threw myself into a new life of meditation and spiritual development. I felt that I wanted to repay the power that had answered my prayers by dedicating my life to working for it. I joined a group to develop my healing more fully, a sort of prayer-without-words, a meditating group, and on my first sitting, even though I had my eyes closed, I saw in my inner vision the nun I talked about earlier standing behind me. I never mentioned this to the rest of the group, but only later told my best friend. From that time on – even though I never connected this with my mystery nun – I developed a pain in the shoulder behind which she had appeared, a pain that went from bad to worse. Even though I sought help from many alternative practitioners, the pain increased and gradually spread to my other limbs. But the worst and most noticeable affliction was concentrated in my hands and wrists. My fingers curled and wouldn't straighten and I found I couldn't even sew the tapestries that I normally found so relaxing.

Over the course of the next year, I consulted many prominent doctors and alternative practitioners. At one point I was even diagnosed as having carpal tunnel syndrome and underwent two painful operations to remove my carpal tunnels, operations that left me unable to use my hands for many weeks. (You really know who your friends are at a time like that, as I couldn't even use the toilet on my own.) But when the bandages finally were removed, the condition had not changed; the cause had still not been found.

Finally, after many more tests, I found myself sitting in front of a huge, elegant, antique Harley Street desk, which I felt after all my treatments I had probably paid for, looking at the top of my latest specialist's head as he pondered my notes and announced that I had arthritis. 'Thank God,' I thought, 'at last I can be treated!' But I was dismayed to be told that I would be started off on aspirin, and when they could no longer control the pain, I would be upgraded to another drug. He was telling me I would be drugged for life!

Now all the time I had been on my search for a cure I had been in contact with a medium who had, in fact, helped me enormously. She had brought to me messages from my mother on the other side and had told me that I had a very important role to play in this life. It had been strange the way she had come into my life. I had been helping a girl friend who was suffering badly in many ways and she had heard of this medium and had written to her. Then one day she had reached her wit's end and felt her life had broken down. She lay on her bed in despair and had asked for help and – yes, you've guessed it – the phone rang and it was this lady telling her that she had been pushed to ring her right at that moment. That very call in itself was healing for my friend and gave her great hope, so she agreed to go and visit this lady. The medium lived a long way away, however, so I drove her to her appointment to keep her company. But instead of being told to wait outside, as I expected, the lady talked with my friend and then turned her attention to me. She said that she knew she had to help me on my path and that the work I would do would benefit many people. At the time I took this with a pinch of salt, but from then onwards for a long time she would ring out of the blue every time I felt I had lost the path. She also took me to meet another medium who was a trance worker. She also worked with me and actually brought about my spiritual development in that area, and is still a close friend and helper.

The only trouble with my new helper was that she was so immersed in the non-physical that I had affectionately nick-named her Madame Arcati. She had kept telling me I was suffering from a past-life condition, but this had often annoyed me and I just ignored her and thought, 'I'm in pain, please don't give me all this airy fairy rubbish,' and so avoided her. But when told of the threat of being drugged for life I decided I had nothing to lose. Madame Arcati here I come!

And so there I was. The regression in which I experienced my life as Sister Theresa had taken just over half an hour, my pain had gone and my fingers were straight. It explained so much. Not only the painful arthritis but, on reflection, why I had suffered throughout my present life from an unnatural fear of surgical instruments. As a child I would become hysterical when confronted with any such things. In fact, one of my earliest memories is of being taken to hospital with a suspected mastoid in my ear and the still very clear recollection of seeing a neat row of gleaming surgical paraphernalia, which resulted in me having to be held down while the doctor merely used his light instrument to examine me.

I also had terror attacks near dentists. I know that this used to be a very common thing, but at school the dentists at least used to use gas to knock us out before taking out a tooth. On my first visit to a dentist after I had left school, I totally embarrassed my mother when the dentist only froze the gum, leaving me wide awake. I attacked him with such ferocity that he ended up lying on the ground with tool still in hand as I ran for the door and made my escape. I have even fainted as dentists approached me. It was only when I discovered today's modern knock-out injections that this aspect of my present personality was cured. I also have a loathing for dark Spanish-style furniture and have even been known to change hotel rooms because of the deep feeling of fear that it creates. At least I now understand these aspects of my personality and can live my life around these aversions.

In telling you about this cure for my arthritis I am not advocating that anyone who is ill should rush out and expect a miracle past-life cure, I'm simply telling you how it happened to me. I don't feel that I am a normal case because I know that what happened to me happened in order to seal my convictions. I have now been working as a healer, counsellor and regressional therapist for over twenty years, and I feel that my amazing experience was meant to happen as a means of giving me strength to carry out this work.

Our soul memories are only memories and could easily be thought of as imagination by some people. To be good at my work I have to have complete faith in what I do; that is the only way to bring through the power to take my clients to see the times they have spent in the past. As a result of my experience, I have this faith, and even on my wobbly days I can cast my memory back to the proof I had of one of my past lives, and carry on in the face of the most ferocious knock-backs! So firm are my convictions that they have carried me through my whole life up to now with a feeling of security in the future. I know that we are all looked after and just have to go through each of life's experiences for our own learning and growth. In the same way that I was healed by my past-life regression, I use regression as an extension of healing and have been able to remove many fears, phobias and pains from many of my clients over the years.

To achieve this, I never use hypnosis but instead a form of meditation. In fact, I use the same power that comes through when practising hands-on healing. This way the sitter sees for themselves the life being brought forward from their soul memory and knows that it was not trance-induced; after all it is in their memory, not mine.

So, I carried on my work and my development. The more people I treated, the more fascinated I became, and the more sure of my path in life, and though I could talk at great length on this subject, that is not the aim of this book. The aim is to present to you a cross-section of regression cases to give you an insight into how and what can be achieved, and to let you form your own conclusions.

I'll give you an example to show you how it can work. One lady came to me who was convinced that she always carried a bad odour around with her. Although this was not, in fact, true, her fear stopped her from leading a normal life and gave her a terrible complex. Through meditation, I put her back to a memory of a life where she had died in filth and stench, locked up in a prison cell for something she had not done. This soul memory was trapped with her and was responsible for her phobia. It was all in the mind, all a memory, but such a vivid one that it held power to affect her present life. After she understood the source of her irrational fears, she was able to overcome them.

Another example is of a lady who could not touch buttons. As you can imagine, it was a most irritating phobia as all her clothes had to have the buttons replaced by Velcro! When she was regressed she saw a life where she had been a young servant girl in a large house. She had been sexually abused by her master and had consequently become pregnant by him. Of course, she was then sent away to a charity home where she remained for the rest of her life, working sewing buttons onto men's night shirts, hence her aversion to them.

Since the regression she has slowly become more able to cope with the whole thing.

How many times in this life do you sense something – perhaps a tune, perhaps a smell – that instantly throws you back in time? This may, of course, be part of a memory of this life, but it is often in response to a soul memory. In my own life I have often been reminded of things I did when I was younger but which I have completely forgotten. For example, a close school friend who looked me up a few years ago mentioned that I had been her bridesmaid. I was amazed as I still can't remember the wedding, although she produced her photo album and there I was alongside another bridesmaid I would have sworn I'd never met. If one can forget something as close as an event in the present incarnation, then it is not surprising that we cannot easily remember our past lives and this incident showed me how quirky the memory really is. I felt that if an important memory like that could be tucked away in this present mind, how could we doubt that there is much, much more to be discovered?

With each person who comes to me, I generally do a series of regressions which help them to understand themselves and discover where their tastes, desires, styles and drives come from. I have also found that if they had developed a talent or had a gift in a previous incarnation that this, at the right time, can be brought forward again. I believe this goes some way towards explaining people's different aptitudes for learning. I often find that specific examples help to explain an idea. In this case, I am reminded of the autistic boy who made headlines in London, England, because of his astonishing gift of being able just to look at a building as complex as the Houses of Parliament at Westminster, and then sit down and draw it perfectly from memory. He will continue to be the subject of study and controversy; but as you would expect, I have my theories.

So back to the theme of this book. When did it start? About ten years ago I was asked to regress the actor Tom Conti for a feature in the London *Daily Mail*. The intention was to try to cast some light on why he had a mental block when it came to reading music. He loved to play the piano but had never mastered the reading of the dots. I was, of course, aware that one short session would not cure this, but thought it would be an interesting experience so agreed to do it.

Tom Conti himself didn't even think he would be able to see any past lives at all, so we both approached my consulting room with mixed feelings. I felt more tense and pressured than I normally did, as I was being asked to work in such abnormal conditions. For one thing, there was a journalist and a photographer waiting outside, and secondly I was working with a person who had not come to see me of his own volition. However, neither of us should have worried as the regression went very smoothly.

Tom first saw himself as a little boy dressed in a blue velvet suit with a white lace-collared blouse, very much like the famous painting 'The Boy in Blue'. He saw the house he lived in, which was palatial with beautiful gardens. Then I took him forward to see the same boy grown to a man. He was in a large music room, but instead of stopping at the piano (which we both expected him to do) he walked straight past it and took up his position at the harp! (Maybe, we both thought, his trouble was that he had chosen the wrong instrument this time.) He was later quoted in the article as saying of the experience,

> 'I first became a seven-year-old boy, then a leisured land-owning gentleman playing the harp in the corner of a grandly furnished room. It was very clear. I had a completely vivid image of myself as a seven-year-old sitting on a staircase and seeing a little vase of dead daffodils.'

After this experience I was asked by yet another journalist to regress six well-known disc jockeys. I presume that this was for the publicity as at that time I was married to a well-known disc jockey myself. I agreed, and ended up regressing BBC Radio 1 DJs: David Hamilton, Simon Bates, Tony Blackburn, Alan Freeman, Paul Gambachini and Ed Stewart.

As an example of the success of this project, here are some of these regressions. In those days I only put my subjects into one life, whereas now I try to take them to at least two to give a wider idea of the broad nature of their soul memories. Two of the celebrities had their own newspaper columns at that time, so I'll repeat here their own versions of events. David Hamilton wrote:

'Through a process of meditation, not hypnosis, Lee took me back to a time when I was a soldier on horseback fighting in a war. I was able to describe clearly the uniform I was wearing, the enemy – primitive-looking people in long white robes fighting on foot brandishing large swords – and even the sandy, barren terrain. The description was so clear that we were able to pinpoint the time and place where all this happened and that I was a Tira in the British expeditionary force fighting Sudanese tribesmen. I was even able to describe the rest of the family and the house we lived in.'

I remember David's regression well because he was so surprised at the vividness with which he could see the house, with all the family portraits of past military ancestors hanging on the walls up the staircase. Strangely, David's long-standing girlfriend told me she has always called him her little soldier! Perhaps she had been in that life with him, too, as it is often the case that people come together again in many lifetimes. How often have you heard someone say they think they've met someone before? I even had a client who brought me a photograph of her new-born baby and declared that she knew she had known the child before and that she felt right from the first look that the baby looked at her in hate! Much more to come on that subject later.

Simon Bates wrote in his *Daily Star* column:

'I wasn't convinced when I trotted along to Lee's place to be put into regression that I'd find any undiscovered skeletons in my cupboard. There were no tricks, no strange lights, no unearthly voices. I just had a nice cup of tea, a few minutes relaxation with my eyes closed, then suddenly I could feel – almost touch – something quite unpleasant. Under Lee's calming questioning I found myself spilling the beans about a man I knew nothing about and who had lived one hundred years ago. The bloke who turned up in my subconscious turned out to have been a highly successful businessman living near Manchester and . . . nasty wasn't the word for it. This man did everyone out of their savings and seems to have had a well-deserved, miserable existence. Whether or not this unpleasant piece of work really existed, I don't know (I'm looking through the parish records right now), but one thing Lee got right was the way I felt as I left her – like a weight had been lifted from my mind, and all this without the aid of a broomstick.'

All I can add to this is that Simon obviously got being horrid out of his system in that distant life because he's a hell of a nice guy now.

One more fascinating life was that of Paul Gambaccini. He recalled that he had been a priest in the Salem area of Massachusetts.

He saw clearly his tiny one-room church that had been built by the congregation. He saw himself visiting his parishioners dressed in his dark-vested suit. He knew his father had been a settler and had been killed in the process. He had had to work hard to help his widowed mother chopping wood and doing chores, and he had been religious in an optimistic kind of way. But as a priest he had been expected to participate in the inquisitorial witch hunts as a means of purifying the community. Knowing the victims to be innocent people, he had refused to support the witch hunts and had chosen to be defrocked.

He became a writer for a short time, working on a humanist treatise, to try to justify and explain his position, but as the inquisitors gained power he lost his purpose in life and knew that he had thereby lost his will to live. When he finally realised he was near the point of death, he put on his overcoat and a hat (a hat he described as one he associated with turkey hunting) and walked out through the woods to lie down amongst the beautiful autumn leaves and die peacefully. As he passed over he felt redeemed and knew that he was right to stick by his beliefs.

After the session, Paul told me that he goes back to America, where he was born and brought up, almost every year – rather like a pilgrimage – to see the autumn leaves fall, as this is his favourite sight in the whole of nature. He also mentioned that the colour and style of the furniture he saw in the regression (dark brown wood) is his taste to this day and he has his present home furnished this way even down to the wall hangings. In this present incarnation, he was brought up a Catholic, which he took to the extreme and was a fanatic until the age of sixteen when he suddenly stopped following that path. He was, however, never drawn to the cloth, even though he was so devout, as he always felt he couldn't deal with the isolation of the priesthood. He had said during the regression that the isolation was the most painful part of the Salem life. But he did keep up the last habit he acquired in that life: he still loves to write.

So my work as a regressional therapist continued, and the more I did, the more I realised how much influence on this life comes from far memory, soul memory. And because many of my friends are celebrities, I decided to carry on regressing well-known people, along with my other clients, in order to demonstrate this influence. I have now worked with many celebrities, taking each of them back into one or more lives so that we can see what drives them, and perhaps what helped them to where they are today. And because they are famous and people know about their present lives, it is easier to see how they may have been influenced by who they were in the past. Anyway, I do hope this book gives you food for thought.

The regressions in this book took over six years to get together as I often lost heart in the project when it became difficult. Even though I know many famous people, it can still be very hard to get them to agree to do a regression, as it is a very personal experience, so I am doubly grateful to all those who agreed to be included in the book.

But I finally found the urge to go ahead and write this tome, and as I was almost at the final chapter, I saw a television programme featuring a regression done for the camera using hypnosis. The programme was interesting in that it confirmed many of my long-held beliefs.

The subject was the model and actress Paula Hamilton. During her regression, she described herself as a man in the year 1800 and told of her life in fascinating detail. For the climax of this show they had sent out a historical researcher to search for this person that Paula had described. The researcher discovered that all the facts given were correct, even down to the most unusual details which Paula could never have known. For example, Paula described how she had sailed to

Dublin from the port of Parkgate in England. Parkgate is now dry land, but in 1800 was, in fact, a port for ships sailing to Ireland. She described herself as a baker by trade, and added afterwards that she makes her own bread in this life, which is not the most common pastime nowadays.

An interesting part of this demonstration for me personally was the fact that the hypnotist took an hour before getting Paula into her past life. I don't know whether that is normal but I suppose it is necessary to take that amount of time to get the subject into as deep a state as they have to go for their purpose. The hypnotic state is deeper than a meditative state. Like a modern anaesthetic, it can take you just 'under' or deeper if need be. This emphasised to me more fully the power of the light that I work with, as my subjects are never in trance and I generally take them into the life in about ten minutes flat, although they rarely achieve the deepness that brings forward names, times and places. For my work we are not searching for that; we are not trying to prove anything, just to heal. So my clients can remember clearly, as if it were last week or maybe last year, while a hypnotist must tell the subject what they have remembered or play them a tape after the session. Of course, there are a very few subjects who can only be taken to an appropriate state with the use of hypnosis, as you'll see later in this book when I describe a couple of subjects that I didn't manage to take to a past life.

The one thing that worried me with this particular television programme, though, was Paula's description of her death from that life. She died of pneumonia brought about by inhaling flour over long years, but she died in extreme grief for the earlier loss of her wife and stated on her death bed that she no longer wanted to live without her partner. In a later newspaper article she claimed to have felt very sad for days afterwards. Had she been regressed on a spiritual level, she would have been taken into the light and been reunited with her loved one, thus being left feeling secure and happy. I felt this experiment illustrated many of my worries over some methods of regression. The trouble with this approach is that it concentrates on the mind in isolation from the spirit. To take someone deep into their own psyche, ignoring the spiritual dimension, can be dangerous. Mind, body and spirit should be in harmony by the end of the regression.

Interestingly enough, I had had a call from two radio stations before this particular television show was aired and was asked to go on the air and comment on this type of show. Each time I told them that I thought it was not the right thing to do as I felt that if the person taking the subject back in time did not understand or work on a spiritual level, the subject could be left attached slightly to something in that life that should have been cleared. As an example of this, I said that if she had had a limp in that life she could even retain the memory of it in this one. I was right in a way, but in this case what was brought into this life from the past one was grief and sadness.

I must add, though, that I was thrilled that the proof of past existence came over in such a positive way in the programme, and I hope this will lead to more understanding of regression, the kind of understanding I am trying to establish through this book. In any case it certainly looks as though the powers in the sky feel the time is right for the acceptance of past-life therapy, and in that case I am happy about it. What a difference it will make if people realise that this life is not the only one and that there is no death and that all we do rebounds upon us. If we could only make today's hooligans and thugs understand that what they do now will have to be paid for later, the streets would become much safer for us all. Not only do we pay for what we do, but both our deeds and even our thoughts are powerful and can travel. Anyway, I am now left feeling that there is some light at the end of the tunnel in this world. Maybe this new understanding will mark the beginning of things getting better and make some of us think before we act. Mind you, I'm not holding my breath just yet.

❖

CHAPTER TWO

To Help You Understand

Before I go any further with this book, I would like to explain more fully how my regressions are done and clarify some of the expressions I will be using. I feel the best way to do this is to give you a brief history of how I came to be in this work, although I have always thought it is more a 'calling' than a job.

I have already told you that as a child I believed in past lives. I was also very psychic. Although at the time I did not understand it, I now realise that my psychic powers were considerable. My family became accustomed to some of my weird statements. I often talked about past life – much to everyone's amazement – and gave practical examples of past-life knowledge. For example, on one occasion when out in the wilds of the Yorkshire Moors I led my family to a remote tea house. It was a rambling place, but I instantly knew the layout and was able to guide them through it. My sister thought I must have been there before but I knew I hadn't, even though I felt I knew the place so well! I was also extremely sensitive to the extent that if something was wrong I could pick up on it immediately and would weep without knowing why. I had many premonitions and dreams that came true, and grew used to them.

One night I dreamt that I was on the back of a sledge behind a boy at school, a boy I hardly ever mixed with and didn't really like. We came speeding down the very hilly street where I lived and shot up on to the roof of the stables at the end of the road. The boy fell over the edge of the roof, and as I looked down all I could see was a fast-spreading blood stain in the snow. This whole thing seemed to be in vivid Technicolor. Next morning as we were walking to school, I told my mother and my friends about my dream, as I just could not get the vision out of my mind. When we arrived in our classroom, the boy in question was not there and later the teacher informed us that he had had a very bad accident on his bicycle the night before. He had run into the back of a lorry, crushing his head. He never again returned to school. That vision of spreading blood recurred every night for weeks and made me quite fearful of going to bed.

In later years I learned through regression that I had been in a life before with this same boy. His actions in that life meant that he owed me a karmic debt – a debt which would be held over into other lifetimes until it was repaid – and which in this case was repaid in a way that helped me on my spiritual path.

I was shown a life where I was a shaman in a Red Indian tribe called the Cree in Canada, and at the end of that life, the tribe were under threat from the white men. The chief asked me to consult the spirit guides, which I did by grinding up stones, throwing the dust into the fire and reading the shadows on the sides of the wigwam. I remember that the fact that I saw the fire inside the wigwam convinced me of its authenticity as I had not realised that they built fires inside the tents. I was later to meet this chief, my blood brother, and work with him in this present incarnation, as I describe later on. The spirits told me that we should take the tribe and move on to safety, which we the elders agreed upon. But one of the young braves held a meeting with the other young braves and roused them into war mood. He led all our youths and our future out to their deaths, leaving us destitute. The chief and I went out to the battle ground to collect the bodies and they were all lying in huge red blood stains in the snow. At the end of the regression when I was taken into the light, I was shown the whole tribe back together again and there was the young brave who went against my advice. As I looked at him he changed into the very boy whom I had seen in my dream twenty odd years earlier. I was startled at this and said, 'My God, it's Michael'.

Later, when at home, the words 'Malcolm, Malcolm' went round and round in my head until I realised that my mind memory had got it wrong; the boy's name was, in fact, Malcolm. He had shown me what my spiritual hearing was and how to recognise it, how to distinguish it from ordinary thought patterns. He had corrected me in my mistake with his name, which helped me enormously in my future work. He owed me a debt from the Cree life and had made a start by helping my work in this life.

Just as that particular regression was brought to me at the right time in this life, many more lives were shown to me as my work grew and as the memories were needed. I realised more and more that the work I had chosen in this lifetime was only a continuation of the work I had undertaken in previous incarnations.

As an extremely sensitive child, I was protected throughout my upbringing by the most loving and caring parents; we were a very close-knit family. My mother had a marvellous soprano voice that rang out clearly on washing day – everyone washed on Mondays at that time. Mam had been offered management to become a professional singer when she was young but my father – although a wonderful man – was a strict Victorian who did not believe in women working after they were married. He treated all his three girls – Mam, myself and my older sister Brenda – as though we were rare bone china.

I think Mam always regretted not going on the stage. Singing had run in the family as her mother had been a singer, too; in fact, it was the indirect cause of her death. I never met my grandmother but I was always told that I looked like her and at one time my parents feared that I would follow her fate. She used to sing professionally in public houses but, as the pubs were open all day then, she would be out most of the day singing and being given drinks until she eventually became an alcoholic. While she was out singing, my mother looked after her younger brother and was more or less the woman of the house. One day her apron caught fire as she lifted the kettle off the hob and she ran out into the yard on fire and screaming. A neighbour rushed to dowse the flames with a blanket and he received first degree burns on his hands and arms, so you can imagine how badly burned my mother was. She did, of course, recover, and in fact she never even had any scars – a healing trait that was passed to me too as I heal very quickly – but she was on the danger list for quite a while. My grandmother was so overcome with shame and guilt that she turned teetotal instantly, but the shock to her system was the direct cause of her early death. She died of not drinking. So like my mother and her mother before her I was, I think, born with the desire to be a professional singer and it was inevitable that I would carry on the tradition. I would sneak into my parents' room when they were out, to practise in front of their full-length mirror.

I grew up, however, and did what all good Northern girls did in those early days: got married. At that time, national service was compulsory and most couples married before the call up to get the army pension. In my case it was a mistake, as I suppose many others were, although my husband was a lovely person and I always felt he got a raw deal with me as I had this burning desire to be a musical star. I did eventually get to the stage and worked with big bands and in cabaret and television and even made three records. I suppose I managed to get the singing bug out of my system for myself, my mother and her mother. Mam used to come and see me in cabaret and she would well up with tears of joy and pride. I felt I completed her ambitions too. Through my singing career I met the pop star Billy Fury and I became his common-law wife for the next eight years. After we split up I married the disc jockey and comedian Kenny Everett and that lasted fifteen years until I finally married my present husband, John Alkin, who was at that time an actor. My life story has been published twice. I believe that all the drama I have gone through in my life has given me the empathy for my clients as I have now been working as a healer, spiritual counsellor and regressional therapist for the past twenty-five years. This is my calling in life.

To put a sitter back to seeing a past life I use the same power that comes through me for healing. I never use hypnosis. The subject is fully aware of what is happening at all times. The difference in using this power is that for healing it comes through my hands, but for regression it seems to take my whole body; it even seems to fill the whole room. Generally when counselling it is a similar feeling. When I say 'the power' I'm trying to describe what I call the light. In fact, many clients see the room grow lighter, often seeing it begin by encircling my whole body. Most, however, simply feel a light that seems to bring a stillness and an overpowering sense of peace.

For the past-life work, I'm simply the conductor for the power that brings forward the soul memory of my subject. The soul memory is what we call far memory, memory of lives that are gone. When we are born, the soul enters the new body and part of that soul is the memory of its previous experiences and achievements. When we reach the end of a life, the body stops functioning and the soul, with its now-enlarged memory, passes back into the light. In fact, the soul is made up of light.

The soul and the mind are not the same thing. For some people, it helps to describe the soul as the intuition or the conscience. I teach meditation because I know that so many people expect the mind to be their guide, but the mind is only part of the body and will be buried or cremated with it when this life is over. It's useless expecting the mind to know what to do in difficult situations because it can only solve practical difficulties. If you learn to quieten the mind, then the soul will be your guide. The soul is the part of us that knows why we are here and what we have come to achieve; it is our guiding light and should be our only helper.

Let me give you an example to clarify this. If the telephone rings and I answer it and hear what I feel is bad news, news that seems to be against all my plans and hopes, I would feel that rush of fear that we get in our stomachs when things go wrong. If I give in to that feeling and begin to get worked up, things only get worse. But if I realise that what I heard on the telephone is something my mind does not understand and therefore cannot be expected to deal with, I immediately go somewhere where I can sit alone and make my mind go quiet. It can even be to the toilet if there is nowhere else; anywhere I can be alone. Once I have taken the news away from my mind, my body goes quiet once more and I feel as if someone has said to me, 'That's all right, this has to happen to get you to the next stage'. The soul has reassured me that things have not gone wrong as my mind has said. I then find that I make the new arrangements quite calmly because I have been comforted and reassured. That's because the soul also knows what and where we should be going and doing and even knows the alternative plan for when things have gone astray. I always follow my soul's guidance and have complete confidence in where it leads me. Another word for this is faith; my faith is very strong and stops me panicking easily.

So when I am regressing a subject, I help them to relax into this meditative state where their soul takes over. I generally get them to visualise something like a door, a staircase or a house – anything to get them focused. So if you think it strange that many of the regressions feature doors or staircases, then it is only because I have used them as objects to get the session started. It is the sitter who sees their own past and so relates it to me, as the life is in their memory not mine. I am the catalyst who puts them in touch with their soul. I prompt them through their memory by my questions, and if there is a very unpleasant experience which comes forward during the regression, I am able – by talking and guiding them – to steer them past it so that they feel only the emotion of the experience, not the pain. I know when to steer clients past particular experiences by my instinct; when working I have very clear feelings of when and how I have to push my subject on through the memory.

Some people ask if regression is dangerous. The answer is no. If it is done by a professional it can only be beneficial. For example, my present husband, John Alkin, came to me because he had lost his confidence and needed support and counselling. He was shown a life in which he was very successful, which brought forward the feeling of success and lifted his spirits, feelings he could then transfer to this life. Others come because they either have recurring nightmares or irrational fears and phobias.

Recurring nightmares are often flashes of past memories that have not been cleared. All I do is go into meditation and get my sitter to relax, close their eyes and think of nothing, and then when I get the feeling that all is ready (when again my instinct or guidance urges me to go on) I gently talk to them and ask them to visualise something mundane like a staircase or house. When I know they are seeing clearly, I ask questions that will take them backwards and forwards through the life they are experiencing, while we do a sort of detective work around the life. For example, when they are well into the memory I will ask them where they eat and they generally tell me where they are and who is there with them; that way we find out who else is in the family. If necessary, I ask them where they sleep and have even asked to see what is in the wardrobe to establish whether they are male or female in that life, if they have been reticent about that. I even get them to lead me to a mirror to see what they look like.

The more I get them to wander about in the life, the clearer it becomes, and without realising it they go deeper and deeper into the memory. The beauty of this is that the deeper the subject goes into the memory, the more peaceful they feel when they come out, as being in this state of light and meditation gives them a great feeling of being uplifted, rather as if they have been taken on a restful holiday away from their minds.

During regressions, people may see themselves as a different sex and race, and while some accept this as natural, others fight against it. Many examples of this switching of gender come in later chapters. I even had one black man who, when regressed, found himself to be a white slave trader in an earlier life, in which he was extremely cruel. In his present life, he was finding things very hard, but after his regression he has found that he now understands what he has to do in this life and his feelings of general resentment and anger have gone. I always feel sad when I see a black person who is bitter because of the cruel and terrible activities of the slave traders in the past because – who knows? – that same bitter person could well have been white in that period of time.

The power of the light is what I feel I work for. As you know there are many names for this light; some people call it God. It's the same power as love. When I meditate I see this light quite clearly as the brightest of lights that when brought forward heals, comforts and guides. I know we are all of the light, we are light. I have been called to the bedside of many people when they are dying so have witnessed the passing of many souls. Each time I see the light leave the body. I see this with the naked eye, not inner vision. I know then that even though the body may still be functioning (perhaps with the help of machinery or drugs) the spirit has left and the life is over. I even see these lights around people and know that there is a loved one holding close to them, probably to give comfort. I sometimes see tiny lights bobbing along behind the heel of a person and realise that their beloved pet is visiting, probably because that person is thinking of it. So I know animals have spirits and are with us in the light when we pass through.

I also spent many years doing what we call clearances in houses which are 'haunted', a word I hate because seers like myself (and there are many of us) know that there is a spirit trapped there in the physical world, someone who died perhaps in fear or hate or any of the negative emotions. These negative emotions I see as being in the dark, and as the light cannot enter darkness, someone trained like myself is sent in to help them reach the light. This is what I mean when I talk about guiding people through regression and say, 'I had to release the poor souls into the light'. I have done a clearance from that person's past life and exorcised the actual space where that event took place. It's like travelling back in time to revisit a haunted house at the very moment the spirit became entrapped in it. When I get to the end of a client's life and find they are trapped, usually in the place they died, I use many different ways to get them to the light, depending on how badly they are trapped. Generally I'll use the power of their mind and ask them to imagine they are on a conveyor belt or moving staircase. As they are going up I ask them to look at the bright light that has appeared. They always see it and when they enter it they even feel the warmth of it. Then they start to feel very peaceful and happy as though a great weight has been lifted from them, which of course it has. Often in the light they see relatives who have already passed into the light, so I get to enjoy and be part of many a wonderful reunion. If the life that they have just seen ends very fearfully, I have to resort to many other ways of taking them to the light and they can often be very difficult, but I always succeed. Often the subject cries all the way through the life, either with emotion or sometimes sadness, but that sadness is all over after they enter the light.

For many people, all the things I have just related will be too hard to believe, but looking back over the years I have been in this field there are more and more people having experiences that have made them 'see the light'. In recent years about a dozen books have been published by medical professionals charting the experiences of people who have had Near Death Experiences, or NDEs. They have all been pronounced clinically dead but subsequently recovered, and they all say they went up a long, dark tunnel towards a very bright light and in this light met dear, departed loved ones and sage-like beings. There are few exceptions to this, although one high-profile one was the millionaire cricket promoter who was pronounced dead but recovered to insist that there was nothing but darkness. I believe that he probably was trapped and if he had really died he would have needed a soul rescue by me or some other spiritual worker. It is a wonderful innovation for this type of information to come from the scientific field, as mediums have been working for years to prove the spirit world exists – and been ridiculed for their trouble – and these examples of NDEs are a great help at least in making people more open-minded towards their beliefs. I never try to make people follow my beliefs. If a person is not ready for it, then it is the wrong time and I leave it to fate.

I also feel that the release of a soul into the light is a very valuable thing to do. I see our souls as uncut diamonds and each lifetime is the fashioning of a facet of that jewel. Each time we incarnate we grow spiritually. Often that growing is painful, as we all know, but pain and suffering brings growth and enlightenment. We often learn our lessons by firstly doing things wrong. Those wrong things we do are frequently the things that make us ashamed of ourselves, but this should never be. No one should be ashamed of doing the wrong thing when the very fact that they know it was wrong means they learnt what was right. When each lifetime ends and the soul passes back into the light, it only takes with it what was learned not the misses and mistakes, so when a soul becomes trapped in its darkness it means that the mistakes are still with that soul and can be drawn upon in the next life.

I've seen the attitude to the psychic and spiritual in the world change so very much, even more than I dreamed, over the past thirty years. For example, my work and the work of others as healers is now not only accepted, but we are allowed to practise alongside traditional medicine. We even have our own register, The British Register of Complementary Practitioners, which is run by The Institute of Complementary Medicine. Who knows how long it will be before we see the need for clearances as being as essential as any other form of counselling.

Recently I watched a television show where the victims of a school fire that occurred many years previously, and claimed many lives and ruined others, were reunited to discuss the effects this trauma had had upon them. One lady told of how, after the event, they had all been pushed to another school and made to get on with their lives as if it had never happened. Even though she had lost her own brother in the fire, nothing was discussed again. She told how – because she had not had help – her mind had blocked out the whole thing and she did not even remember being in a fire. But of course this mind block had eventually come forward in nightmares, and when finally her own children were of school age she had an uncontrollable fear for them. So finally, after thirty-five years, she has been given counselling and is now able to deal with the whole experience. This not only speaks volumes for counselling, but shows how we ignore the needs of our soul at our peril.

I did a regression with a lady who had suffered in a similar way. She came to me because she had so many allergies she could hardly enjoy life; there was so little she could cope with. I felt she needed to be taken back to find out where her total allergy syndrome began, but when I put her into the past she only went back to when she was a child in this same lifetime. She remembered for the first time being asleep in bed and being woken by a commotion downstairs. She got up and tiptoed to the top of the stairs to find out what was going on. To her horror, she heard that her beloved older brother had been killed that night in a car accident. Next day, her parents sent her to a relative in Wales to stay for a few months and no one ever told her what had happened to her brother; in fact he was never mentioned again. Her mind was so damaged by this denial of what had happened that she blocked the whole memory out, but in doing this she also made herself very ill. I know from my upbringing in Sheffield that parents often thought it better to not talk of death to children. This can be so dangerous. Children are instinctive and intuitive – often more so than adults – and simply not speaking about something does not take away the fact that it has happened and has affected them. The only course of action to take is to help them face up to what has occurred. Counselling and healing can do this, and so can regression. These illustrations show the value of regression.

One aspect of the media's treatment of regression I find very irritating is the fact that films about past lives invariably make them very full of frightening events which the makers call artistic licence. But, of course, these things stick in people's minds and make them wary of regression. But they give quite the wrong impression. I recently watched a television programme in which they showed a poor woman who, after regression, slipped backwards and forwards from the past to the present, and ended up being murdered in the same way as she had been in the past. At the end, the credits informed us that it was based on a true story. What a load of hogwash! In the last twenty odd years and hundreds of sessions, nothing remotely like that film has happened to any of my clients. No wonder there is so much fear implanted in us.

Just last week I was visited by a woman whose husband had forbidden her from having the regression she wanted. He said that he knew it would change her and he wouldn't allow it. However, she did go against his orders and went through with the session which, of course, allayed not only all her fears but I hope her husband's, too.

The examples I have given show you that when a client comes to see me they very often have a particular problem to deal with, and in these cases, the sittings usually concentrate on the crisis point in the past life which has affected the present one. I can then help the client to work through that event and clear it from their soul memory. For this book I have changed the way I would normally work, as I have tried to talk the subject through their past life to get a fuller picture, to show how much our soul memories can recall and how it can affect present incarnations.

Also when transcribing the descriptions of the lives from the tape recordings I have made, I cut out most of my questions so that the story flows freely. So the fact that they seem pretty straightforward and even perhaps glib is because I have neatened up the sessions to make them readable and accessible. The words have not been changed; the facts have not been altered.

To add a final note, in my work I specialise in the development of future healers. Within this training I take the students back to their past lives, often either to clear a life that didn't go to the light or to bring forward to the physical memory a gift that could be used in this life. This helps to make what I call a clear channel for the light. The development of healers means opening their sensitivity and for that they must become clear channels to survive. By clear channel I mean that they have nothing inside them that would throw them into negativity. For example, if someone feels guilty about some past action, then that guilt gives them vulnerability and makes them throw smoke screens around that area. That means that a false situation is created which could lead to the wrong motive in a statement. It is essential in the healing-counselling field that the motives for everything are pure, or more harm than good could be done. The students have to learn to love themselves so they can love the people who are put before them.

I feel very strongly that this training is of vital importance in my work, because the result is that there are more experienced and sensitive counsellors to guide those who need their help and support, or who want to experience regression. If you want to experience regression, please speak to someone at one of the registers such as The British Register, as I mentioned earlier, and find out about professionally trained therapists so that you are protected from the many charlatans at large, for it pains me to say that there are unscrupulous people out there whose claims are not to be trusted. When done properly, regression is a very lightening and wonderful experience, one that can generally enhance your life by giving you a greater understanding of yourself and often of the people who are with you and around you on your present path. It can also bring a feeling of security in the knowledge that we are looked after, and the wonderful strength imparted by the assurance that the power of love never dies, it only grows. It can also help many people to cope with feelings of grief or fear of loss, as it proves that we will all meet again and that death is not an ending, but a stage on our lives' path.

❖

CHAPTER THREE

Doubting

Thomases

Every time I have seen a programme about regression there have always been at least some people who are convinced that it's all in the imagination of the sitter, and when researching this book I encountered quite a few celebrities who shared that scepticism and felt that either nothing would happen at all, or if it did it would be all fantasy or in the present memory. How many times have you heard people go on about the fact that they were sure that all the things were from the subconscious, things that had been read about in a fictional work or seen in a movie?

One of these doubters was Jimmy Tarbuck, our well-loved comedian and golfer. He rang me to say that he didn't want to upset me by falling about in hysterics in the session but if I didn't mind that, he would be glad to sit for me. I actually pondered on this, as it was early on in this project and I felt that if that was his attitude to it, the session would be a total disaster. I had decided to leave him off my list until my husband pushed me into it by accusing me of being a quitter. So as you can imagine, it was with extreme trepidation that I drove to Jimmy's house on the day of our appointment. Once more I should not have worried. Not only did he not fall about laughing, he really enjoyed the session and mentioned to a friend that he would love to be regressed again! Jimmy has a warmth about him anyway that made the whole session very enjoyable. Here's one of his pasts as he saw it.

'I'm seeing a wooden door, a medieval one: it goes to a point at the top and has silver-coloured studding on it. It's the entrance to a castle that's very baronial on the inside with stone slab flooring and huge tapestries on the walls – one depicts a hunting scene and another is a massive victory with knights in suits of armour. There's a large wooden table with matching chairs in front of a huge fireplace with a roaring fire.

'There's a group of men standing in front of the fireplace dressed like knights but without the armour, they're wearing tabards, I think they are called. They are all drinking. I'm wearing comfy shoes like old-fashioned chukka boots, and some sort of leggings; they are definitely not trousers. One particular man seems to be the centre of attention. He's dressed very casually in white blouson shirt with big sleeves. He's in his thirties; I'm about the same age. There are lots of banners hanging just off the walls all the way down the hall; they have crests on them.

'I sleep in a room that has stone floors and there's a big chest in front of the bed. I spend many of my days with the same group of men. I can see us all on horseback. The horses are dressed up like knights' horses with coloured things over them. We've all got our own falcons and we hunt with them.'

We go forward ten years.

'I'm in a lovely old black and white house and I'm sitting at a table writing something; I'm writing in

English. There's a boy in the room with me, wearing leggings and shirt; I know he's my son. My wife is very pretty and wearing a dress to the floor and a kind of band keeping her hair in place.'

We see him at work.

'I'm on the horse now. We're either side of someone – someone very prominent – there are two of us either side of him, like guards. I think he's the king or at least a lord or something.

'The last day of my life I am with the king, fighting. There's a hill and we are up on top of it. There are archers and I get killed . . .'

At the end of the life when he had seen his death in battle he said he went into a very lovely and peaceful grotto. He felt he was barefoot and wearing a white smock. He felt completely at peace. There were also a few of what he described as Disney-type characters gathered around him. 'I wonder where my mind is,' it made him say. He also told me that it seemed he has always had a liking for the grand life.

Tony Blackburn, the disc jockey and television personality, came to my consulting room quite happily and seemed, apart from being slightly nervous, very open-minded. But as his session will now reveal he only looked as though he thought something would happen. In actual fact – in spite of him seeing one of his past times very clearly – his mind would not let him see himself in the midst of it for ages. But, of course, he finally saw himself in the scene and the whole episode took on another view. Here's his life.

'There's a stately home, it's a big house, very big, in fact it is a stately home!'

I take him inside.

> 'I'm taken by all the pictures and things. I feel it's a place I've been before; I think it's Woburn Abbey; I've stayed there. Mind you, it's not quite the same place, though. There's a minstrels' gallery with long passages and pictures on the walls. I'm not getting anything now, I've lost my way.'

I take him away from this void and out for an aeroplane ride, then have him parachute into space and we wait to see where he lands. I did this to separate him from what he felt was an image of this lifetime, but as you will see he can't get away from it at all.

> 'I'm on the moors in the wilds. There's heather and views. I'm approaching a house – it's the same stately home! I'm on the driveway this time going up to the front door. It's very big and square in appearance; the front of the house is very square. You can drive straight up to the front door. It's a typical stately home like you would see in a film. The drive is loose stone. The front door is very big and impressive, very heavy, very old. The entrance is seriously impressive and the staircase is the same one I saw before; it's in front of me, I'm in the same place! It's very big with armour and stuff all round it. The staircase is to the left-hand side and as you go up it there is that balcony I was describing earlier. It's full of pictures of all the ancestors. I'm walking along the top of the stairs to a room on the left-hand side. For some reason if you come out of this room you would be right on top of the head of the stairs. It's a bedroom, a green room with a big, very old-fashioned bed. There's a window which looks out on to some beautiful

gardens. The house seems to be empty. If you're sitting on the bed, to the right-hand side there's another door that goes into a bathroom. It's weird, this bathroom's really up to date! It's not in keeping with the rest of the house, it's not the same.'

At this point I feel he is still not quite deep enough into the regression to hold him there, and he is still going from past to present. His mind is coming forward and interfering. This only happens occasionally, generally when the sitter is nervous. I carry on and hope he will go deeper. To try to get him to see himself in this place, I ask if there is a mirror.

'Yes, it's in front of the bedroom with an old-fashioned shelf underneath with objects on it. It has a wooden frame that is very decorative and the top of it is carved. I can only see the reflection of the window opposite in it. I'm not there, it's just a window.'

I take him downstairs.

'There's a massive hallway. The armour is like a display thing for people to look around, like a museum. I've come to a heavy wooden door with a doorknob. I've turned the handle to the left and have gone in. It's a thickly carpeted room in a flowery pattern, with old-fashioned furniture. It's another bedroom – this house is full of bedrooms! There's a bed on the right-hand side, it's the same style room but slightly brighter.'

I take him to the kitchen.

'There are people in the kitchen, they're staff, cooks etc. They all seem to be wearing white and it's very old-style clothing. There's a very long kind of stove and somebody is by it in a white hat, an old lady cook. Everyone else has now gone; when I came in they all left. It's weird, it's as if as soon as they saw me they went, as if I'm not supposed to be there. It's rather like being a spirit and just wandering around. The kitchen's a very old one with a sink at the back, a very large sink and this very long thing you cook on is to its right. It's a stone floor and opposite the stove there are pantries with lots of jars and food and packets – it's not neat. There are utensils in them as well, and there's a broom.

'I'm in the dining room now. It's a lovely, beautiful table and the room has chandeliers, lots of old-fashioned wooden chairs, and at the top and other end of the table there are carvers. The table is set for eight people, with wonderful candlesticks in the centre.'

Let's bring the people in.

'The people come from behind me, there's a door there. I'm not there, I'm just observing it. There are children: a little boy and a little girl. She's wearing a very pretty dress, very high in the neck, a long dress, a period dress; it's the horse and carriage era. It's a brother and sister but I'm getting the girl clearer; her dress is in velvet. They are about ten years old and sitting to the left-hand side of the table. For some reason the table settings have gone down to four people.'

Let's bring the rest of the family in.

'The mother is wearing an old-fashioned evening dress. She's a very stately-looking person, very nice.

She looks a very feminine, very upper class lady. She's wearing jewellery and dressed up to the hilt, wearing a beautiful, expensive-looking diamond necklace and the dress is very low cut with the jewellery resting on the front. Her sleeves are puffed up at the top like leg-of-mutton sleeves and narrow down to the wrist, but at the top around the shoulders it's all puffed up; it's a lovely long dress. It's like a film set.'

Are the rest of the family there?

'It seems to be just the children and the mother.'

I try once again to get him to see himself.

'The room at the left has a mirror. There's lots of mirrors and old-fashioned shelves. The room looks out through very big doors on to beautiful grounds. I'm only getting two children and the mother; there doesn't seem to be a father there.'

Can we see the meal served?

'There's a silver cover: the sort of thing that has meat under it.'

Where are you now?

'I'm still observing it. Oh no! I know why I can't see me, I'm sitting at the top of the table!'

I sigh with relief, and ask what he is wearing.

'I still can't see myself, I'm not aware of myself.'

Stick your foot out from under the table and see what shoes you have on.

> 'It's very weird. They're very pointed shoes with buckles on them and gaiter things on my legs, old-fashioned trousers all puffed out, very beautiful, thick, sort of velvety type of things. My jacket has thin lapels and there's frilly lace. I'm very dressed up.'

He bursts into giggles and I join him in relief that he's finally accepted that he's starring in this film.

> 'Round the sleeves of the jacket it's goldish, very loud, and my hands are not the hands of a young person at all. I'm about fiftyish or even more, but the wife is very young and so are the children. I have very thin hands with very long nails – they are not like my hands at all, they're very thin, bonyish and very well manicured, so unlike what I am now. I can see myself – it's weird. I'm wearing one of those old-fashioned powdered wigs. I'm definitely an older man and quite tall and thin. The children are lovely, very well behaved. That is my wife! She's very young – well when I say young, she's about thirty-five-ish but very lovely with beautiful features, a lovely looking lady.'

Tony let out a sigh of extreme satisfaction at this point.

> 'Her hair is very beautiful, it's very curled and sort of lacquered, it's like a wig. The children are giggling a lot, but the table seems too big for us.'

We have gained a lot of information here, so I take him to look at himself earlier in the day.

'I'm in my study reading, still very dressed up, very formal. The room is lovely, I'm sitting on an old-fashioned couch in a beautiful room. Once again it has lovely windows that look out on to countryside. I think I must be very wealthy.'

We go back to the age of twenty.

'I've got a car, an early sort of thing. I can see a car but it's completely out of context with what I've seen before.'

I realise I have lost him as he has moved to another lifetime. I try to get him back to when he was ten years old.

'I can see my mother now. She has a picnic basket, and she's wearing very heavy tweedy stuff with a hat on, a very old-fashioned square thing just balanced on top of her head. We're out in the countryside with ferns and things. I'm wearing trousers and a jumper.'

I take him back to the house to try to get him back to the first life he saw.

'Yes, it's the same house but I have gone back to the picnic and my mother is standing over me. She's very tall, or maybe she looks tall because I am so small. She has a big cape on and this basket thing. She opens the basket and all the things are wrapped up, sandwiches and things. She's opened up a blanket to sit on and is putting all the things on the floor. The basket is wooden, like a hamper with a big handle that goes from one side to the other. It's a very big basket for two people. At the end of the picnic we are getting into the car, it's an old-fashioned thing like a Rolls-Royce. It's got mudguards at the front and a spare wheel at the back. It's a beautiful car of it's time, an open car, almost like a 'Chitty Chitty Bang Bang', a four-seater with a hood that can be drawn over it. There's a chauffeur driving it and I'm sitting to the left-hand side of my mother in the back. The chauffeur is dressed very smartly, and we're driving up to the house. The chauffeur drives the car away and we go into the house.'

This session had already taken a lot longer than my normal sessions and time was getting short as we both had further appointments, so I decided to let him finish the second life. Later on, when my mind was clear, I thought about the very unusual situation that had occurred, and it would appear that he probably had had two lives in the same place. When asked to drop by parachute, he had seen the same fern and countryside as his picnic place. I asked him where his father was.

'In the study. He's dressed in Pickwick-type clothes. The trousers sort of go into his socks like plus fours, he doesn't look anything like my own father used to be. He's got a moustache and I don't like him, his face is not kind. I don't think he works, he's just terribly well off; I suppose he inherited it. He's an older man about fifty. He looks well fed and has a very wrinkled face, but not a kind face.'

I ask him to tell me about his marriage to see if he sees a different woman to the one in the first life. The trouble is that with the confusion with Tony, my mind is also coming back to see logic in this highly unusual scenario. But I feel the power is waning with the effort.

'It's a little church. I can see a woman in a beautiful wedding gown getting out of this car and going into this small church; she looks very lovely. I'm now outside the church with lots of people. We've just got married. She has a white dress and veil and I can't see what I'm wearing, I'm just there. It's a covered car.'

We go back to where he came in.

'It's very easy. I don't seem to be anything, I just seem to be from an extremely wealthy family. It's rather like just living in this massive great, beautiful house with great grounds and I'm very much in love with my wife and the children.'

We go forward to when he was sixty years old.

'The children have gone but my wife is still with me; she's still lovely, just older that's all. She's now wearing the same sort of stuff my mother wore.'

We move on to just before his death.

'I'm in a room in the bed alone. I can see myself! – I'm looking at myself!'

He is obviously floating out of his body in preparation for death.

'The bed's a four-poster and I'm now lying down and look very white. I look as if I've got one of those night caps on. There's a nurse there.'

We move on to the moment of his death.

'I'm still there sort of hovering around the room. I just feel part of nothing at the moment.'

I guided him to the light with difficulty as he could see it but not quite reach it for a while. I felt he didn't want to leave his wife.

'I feel very well now.'

I think Tony is an excellent example of the way the mind sometimes tries not to recognise the past lives, showing that he never really believed that anything would happen at all. It was also very interesting to see that both of those past lives were devoted to his wife and family as he has tried to follow that pattern in this life. He was publicly devastated when his first marriage to Tessa Wyatt broke down and he took a long time to get over it, but happily he seems to have found what he needed now.

Another doubter was Ian Lavender, the marvellous actor who has never quite escaped from his role as that 'stupid boy' Pike in the long-running television comedy *Dads' Army*. He is an old friend and agreed to sit purely as a favour, without believing anything would happen. In the end, I had a tussle as to what chapter to feature him in as he was so frighteningly nervous of the whole thing that I thought at one point I would place his regression in the chapter on fears! It was a very difficult session as his fear made his mind come forward often into his soul memory and question everything that happened, so it was with even more satisfaction that I managed to get him into any past life at all. In fact, he saw himself in these two lives.

'There's a wooden door with two fluted columns on either side; I have never seen this door before. Behind it there's a large hall. It has to be large to accommodate the wide clothing they wore. It's a

large Georgian house. There's a staircase leading up
to the right-hand side. I'm wearing boots, a sort of
riding boot, not the full size ones just small with
breeches. (Am I making this up? It's very similar to
what I was wearing in *She Stoops to Conquer*.) The
hand that is holding the banister is that of a man
and he's wearing black gloves. The jacket is in
three colours and again very similar to the costume
in the play.'

As we were on the stairs, I then asked him to show me his
bedroom.

'Well, I wanted to turn left before and had already
started that way but as soon as you asked me where
the bedroom was, I instantly turned to the right.
Isn't that weird, I knew where the bedroom was!
It's too easy to say but I can see a Georgian four-
poster bed. There's a window but it faces a wall. I
wanted and expected to see a square like the ones
in Bath, but there's only a wall.'

He then goes back to turn left where he originally felt he was
heading.

'It's a very short landing and there's a door; it's sort
of like the front door with the fluted flat column,
and it goes into a sitting room. I know this sounds
stupid, but it's either empty or it's full. Ah yes, now
I can see a desk and a wing chair, there's a
fireplace, I know, but I can't see it.

'I'm a fish merchant! I know it's not exactly a
fit picture but I know I'm a merchant dealing in
fish.

'The dining room is to the left in the big hall;
it's awfully elegant. There are about half a dozen

people and I am placed at the side of the table. There's someone at the head of the table but I can't quite make them out. The door was opened for me by someone else when I entered the room. I'm about twenty years old and my father is also a fish merchant.

'By the time I'm thirty I'm at the head of the table and my father has gone. The others at the table are now my family.'

I question him to see if it is still the same house.

'No, it's cold outside and we are no longer in the city. There are fir trees. I think the big three-floored town house was my parents' home. The house I'm now in is mine.

'At the end of my life I'm in the big house. I know I'm resisting, seeing anything because I'm afraid of death, I'm afraid of being alone.'

I visualised light around him and put him straight towards his next memory.

'At first I saw the sweeping stone staircase that I saw before; in fact, I saw three staircases instantly. But now I can only see some little wooden garretty steps: they are very poor, backstage-types, up-into-attic types. There's one set of steps, again they're leading down on my left-hand side, the hand rail is wooden and rounded and up against the wall. It's very well worn and it seems to go up to a sort of hole. It's an organ loft – it goes up behind an organ. Why do I think it's an organ loft? I'm sure it is, though. I'm sort of crawling up the stairs like a child does. I'm wearing a brown jerkin thing made out of horsehair cloth and I'm not wearing shoes.

It's very urchin style, very poor. There's straw on the floor in the loft and it's very small. I sleep there, I live there, it's cupboardy but it's cosy. I eat at a big trestle table with a lot of other kids; it's like a workhouse.

'Two years later I'm in charge of a group of lads at the dining table. I've got shoes now and I'm sort of a table monitor. It's not a workhouse now. It's similar in style but there's no work, just schooling.

'By the time I'm fifteen I'm on the top table at the top of the hall. I've been there a long time. I'm wearing a coat now made of a much smoother material.

'By the age of twenty I've left the school and I'm seeing lots of water. I'm by a canal at a lock. It's an old-fashioned type of lock and I have to wind the shutters up and down. There's a little house by it. I mostly take my meals outside with two or three people and we sit under a large tree, I seem to work with these people.

'I die before I'm thirty. Again I don't want to see it but my last memory is sitting up against a tree.'

I did manage to get him to see the light this time. We both felt sure that he drowned in this life. Most people who are regressed tend to feel at one point or another that they are imagining the whole thing. Ian felt this even more than most because he is a nervous type of person, but he was convinced of the reality of the memories – like many others – because of the fact that he could always answer specific questions and knew where certain things were or what was happening in the memory. When asked a sudden question, the conscious mind does not get the chance to leap in, and this helps the pictures to flow better.

This session was particularly hard, and I felt sorry for Ian because right next to the room we sat in some builders arrived mid-session and drilled unmercifully at a high-pitched tone! Even so we managed to get what we did. He loved the feeling of meditation that came as the lives finished (the feeling of the light) and said he felt more peaceful than he had ever done. I have promised to teach him how to meditate so that he can make it part of his future life.

His overwhelming fear of death stopped us actually seeing how he died, but I hope that from now on when he thinks of dying he remembers the wonderful peaceful feeling that he experienced when I guided him to the light.

From the numerous regressions I have done with actors and actresses, though, I have found that they have all had trouble sorting out the roles they have played on the stage or on screen from their past. Often, the two overlap, which can cause confusion. A good example of this was my next subject.

Kieth Michell is a wonderful actor who is best remembered for his role as Henry VIII in the television series. He was not a doubter in the straightforward sense, but his session was interesting in that it illustrated how a subject's expectations can make them imagine they know what will happen, with interesting results. I regressed him in his studio in London and the very first memory shows very well both how light a state of meditation we are in, and how wrong his thoughts were about what would occur. I went through three lives with him in all; here's the first one in full.

> 'There's a large Tudor house with square-headed windows. It's all in red brick and there are steps up to the door. I'm standing in a Tudor hall, where there's a big staircase with oak banisters. It's like all the sets I've been on – I feel I've fallen into a trap! It's a modest house. There's a large leaded window at the top of the stairs. I'm wearing square shoes and Elizabethan costume. There's a large tapestry with hounds on it – it looks like one I saw

in New York. I'm at the top of the stairs now and
there are two doors on the left-hand side. I sleep in
a room straight ahead of me. There's a four-poster
bed, a window and a cupboard on the right-hand
side. There's a nice view of fields and a lawn out of
the window, a very English or Welsh type of view. I
fear it's Henry VIII – as soon as I saw the feet I felt
it was.'

Let's see if we can separate a near memory from a far one.
Where do you eat?

'There's a long dining table.'

Where do you sit?

'At the head of the table of course!'

Let's see you sitting down then. Where are you?

'I'm at the side, in the middle opposite the
window. I suppose thinking I was at the head of
the table was just me being grandiose.'

Who else is there?

'The usual bunch of extras!'

We both collapse in fits of laughter!

'I seem to work on a farm. I stand around being
bossy, I think. I do some work. There are horses,
nice ones and working ones. I'm wearing
something plain, it's a sort of golden browny weave
stuff in cotton, or it could be wool; it's very plain. I
think I'm about forty years old.'

You're definitely not ruling the land then?

> 'It certainly doesn't look like it. I've got a scythe
> and a gun. I'm working with the scythe in the
> fields. There are other people there, too. I use the
> gun for game, hunting on foot. I often eat at the
> local inn.'

We go towards the end of the life.

> 'I've got a beard and I'm being nice to people. I
> think it's the family: sons and daughters. I'm not in
> the big house I first saw, I'm in a small cottage
> with white walls. It's very conventional.'

I persuade him to move towards his death.

> 'Oh dear! I'm getting myself all tangled up with the
> Henry VIII series again.'

Are you in the same bed as the film set?

> 'Similar, but it's definitely not the same character. I
> just stop breathing.'

He floats straight to the light.

I liked this particular session because it demonstrated
how close the mind is to the inner memory. The fact that I had
brought forward this memory made it more powerful, but it
does make you realise how close all our lives are at all
times.

By the time we launched into the second life, Kieth had
gone much deeper into the peace of it all and his next two lives
followed in quick succession. Again I'll relay it just as it
happened, warts and all.

'There's a white-washed cottage; it's very nice, it's by the sea. It's quite dark inside and has a simple wooden staircase. It's just like pub furnishing. I've a strong feeling it's Cornwall. The staircase isn't very wide, it's dark wood with banisters in the same wood and it's on the right-hand side of the hall. I'm wearing boots, riding boots. I'm in sort of Jacobean clothes like I've worn in a lot of films.'

At this point the telephone rang, shocking us out of our journey and violently catapulting us back to the present. I usually take it off the hook before I start a session so that I'm not interrupted. Kieth finished with his call and we sat back to resume. He tells me he hopes we can pick up on a life he feels sure he lived in France, which he really wanted to see. I have to explain that it's never my choice what comes through, it's totally out of my hands. We begin again.

'I'm still wearing boots. They look like gamekeeper's boots with trousers, waistcoat and shirt, in sort of browns. It's the same person I saw before the telephone rang. Can we start again? I just don't feel for this person.'

We start again.

'I'm seeing the same cottage.'

I tell Kieth that I realise he doesn't fancy this part and would rather he was given a more interesting one, but as it seems to want to come forward there must be a reason and it should be looked at to clear it. So we once more start again.

'The bedroom's very plain: it's a single room with a small bed but a nice one. I eat downstairs at a medium-size wooden table. My woman is there.

She's in a long skirt and shawl with her hair scraped back and parted in the middle like the Brontë types. She's younger than me, about thirty. We have a couple of boys. I work in the fields and I've got that bloody scythe again! I work on a farm but it's not my own farm.

'By the time I'm fifty-five I'm living in a small country town. I can see myself shopping for bullets. I don't seem to be happy any more. I left my wife and am living at the local inn. We had a row, a very silly reason to leave.

'Five years later I'm on the beach. I'm now working with other men as a fisherman. I don't seem to care much about anything any more. I drown . . .'

I took him to the light and released him.

He seemed to be very tired and felt he had ruined his life. When he had finally drowned he no longer desired to live. Probably the reason he was forced into reliving this life was to clear it forever, as I knew he had died in the darkness of depression and despair.

We then went straight into his next recollection and I'm pleased to report that his French existence came forward this time, but with yet another proof that what one wants to see is not always what one gets.

'There's a lot of ornate gilt. It's like the work in Rome on the altar. It's a sort of palace, a bit like Versailles. I think I've finally got to France! There's a beautiful hall in black and white marble. It's very elegant. The walls are covered in tapestries and paintings. It's like some sort of château.

'I'm wearing a dark waistcoat with shoes, stockings and gaiters or knee-length trousers. I'm also wearing a long wig. I sleep in a nice room:

there's a lot of grey, there's a seascape painting and the view from the window is of an ornate garden with fountains and stuff. I eat in the dining room at the side of the table. There's someone quite grand at the head, he's wearing the lot! There are other grand people there. I'm not dressed particularly grandly, I'm in very drab colours.

'I work as an architect. I'm in an orangery and I seem to be directing the people who are building it. It's very like Versailles. I'm about thirty years old.'

Let's go to the beginning of your career, the first building you worked on.

'It's in Paris, a sort of modest house, mind you it looks a bit Dutch to me. I can see a lot of water, it could be Holland not Paris.'

Let's see your school days.

'Yes, it's Amsterdam. I'm wearing a dark jacket with white shirt and cravat, white stockings and black shoes. The school is some sort of church school with priests and teachers. I eventually studied architecture in a large room with big windows. I studied with much older people. I seem to be an apprentice to one person – he's a nice chap.

'My first work was on a modest church in Holland. I quite like it but I think I'm going to do better. My next project was a house by a canal. It's a bit more grand and I like it but I know I can do better. I then did another house that had lots of glass, about the same level of work as the last house. The next project is a bridge in the country, it's a simple but handsome bridge. I've never done a bridge before and I'm quite pleased with it, but don't feel I want to do another one. The best project I ever did was the first place I saw, the château. I finally made it to Paris.'

We both sigh with relief.

'I'm looking at my drawing of the house, it's of the chimneys. I appear to be working on the whole thing. I'm in my thirties. I'm seeing the place finished now – it's magnificent and I'm more than pleased with myself.

'I live in a nice house in the suburbs of Paris. I have a family and I'm very happy. I'm about sixty now and am quite well but am retired. My greatest achievement was the palace, it seems to be Versailles, it wasn't a château it was a palatsa!'

He did not see his death but I felt him float off happily to the light, so did not press him further. I don't know if it was Versailles, but it was certainly very splendid in his vision. I left him after we had tea and he converted me to using miso – a Japanese soya bean condiment. He has had his own macrobiotic cookery book published. When my taxi came he resumed the lovely painting he was working on, there amidst many of his other beautiful and professional-looking paintings, a completely artistic man. As I mused on this last sighting of him, I thought perhaps it was Versailles!

❖

CHAPTER FOUR

Fears

One of the most common reasons for seeking my help is when people experience unnatural fears that have no apparent or obvious cause, so it was not surprising when quite a few reared their ugly heads amongst our personalities.

One of the many interesting ones occurred during my session with our own loveable Wayne Sleep, the dancer and personality who will always be remembered for his stage appearance partnering Diana, Her Royal Highness the Princess of Wales. Having known Wayne for quite some time and knowing that he can be eccentric and unpredictable, I pottered along to his home not knowing what kind of a session I could expect. I was pretty sure, in fact, that he would not turn out to be your average perfect subject. However, I was quite happy to go along and expect to get nowhere – at least I could say that I had tried. How very wrong I was! He was a marvellous subject and I ended up going through not one but four soul memories on the trot. All the lifetimes were wonderfully clear and, just as in this life, definitely not boring! But as I have tried to group together here a few examples of fears, I will tell you first of his fearful soul memory, and relate the other three lives later on, although I can't resist whetting your appetite by letting you know that in one of his past lives he was a vicar.

The life I am about to relate came last in the session and I feel that this seems to have been projected in that order for a reason, as at the end of this one I had to perform what I have come to call a rescue, taking the soul into the light.

> 'I'm standing in front of some wooden steps.
> They're on a wharf beside the River Thames. I'm in
> dark clothes. It's very dark. The steps lead up to a
> warehouse – it's dark inside and very dank. It's
> rather evil; there are sacks all over the place.'

I try to move him and establish where he lives but he can't get away from this place.

> 'I die young here! I'm very threatened by this
> place.'

He was very upset and wanted to stop the session but I explain that he must face this fear so that we could take the soul to the light to clear it away from him forever. He agrees, so we carry on.

> 'Someone is waiting in the dark for me. He lunges
> at me and stabs me. There are two guys. I can see
> the main man's face: he has thick lips on a fat face
> and the other man is just with him.'

At this point I took him into the light. It was quite difficult but we made it.

> 'I'm seeing the same place again now but this time
> it's light. I look much better now: I'm in a light
> suit, it's tweedy, tight round the lower leg and
> ankle. I'm about twenty-five years old and I'm
> quite nice. I'm sitting in the same place but it's
> light now and I've come through the fear. I've got a

stick, too; it has a shiny handle. I'm a bit of a show off.'

I take him back to look at the life to establish how he met his sticky end.

'I'm an accountant living in the centre of London. I live in a flat on the third floor of the building. It's a Dickensian-type place. That seems to be the time. I work in an office; it's very dull and dark but I don't seem to mind at all. I'm quite a happy person. I discover something that is going on that is to do with my accountancy work. It's something illegal. There's a lawyer involved, too. I manage to row myself in on the fiddle. I'm not really a bad man but I find it very exciting. But it all goes terribly wrong. I've arranged a meeting at a warehouse on the river . . .'

Later on over a nice cup of tea we discussed his feelings about what he had just experienced. He said he felt the warehouse murder had had an affect on this life as he is still afraid of the dark and sleeps with a night light. He also has a fear of being attacked and has had his London home completely secured with strong steel bars. These phobias date back as long as he can remember. He was even afraid to go to the outside toilet in the dark in his childhood home, and he also suffered vivid nightmares about the dark for many years and would look under the bed and in the cupboards before he could sleep. He said the regression made sense of why he has always thought someone was about to jump out and attack him. He was quite stunned by the fact that he could still clearly see the fat, thick-lipped face once the regression was over, and laughed when I said, 'Never mind, love, he'll be paying for it somewhere now.'

I believe this fear had stayed with him into this life

because the memory of that attack had been trapped in the darkness of that fear, so consequently could still be drawn upon and affect his current life. He felt that the murdered soul was like him now, as he feel's he's a bit of a jack the lad and most definitely the dandy type, a lover of life and parties. He was amused by the fact that he had discovered such obvious proof that crime does not pay, and maybe that's why in his next life he had returned as a vicar!

That feeling of fear of darkness and enclosed spaces – claustrophobia – is one of the most common of the fears that find their way into my consulting room. I actually used to have a recurring dream of having to crawl through a tunnel and would wake up sweating. However, since seeing a life when I was buried alive in a landslide, the dream has just faded away. Strangely enough I haven't really thought of it until writing this book, but now I realise that I had a clearance then. I think many cases of claustrophobia could be traced to a past life, unless the phobia can be explained away in this life, of course. One of my clients came to me because she was getting panic attacks that were affecting her breathing. She thought that she was developing asthma, until I took her into a life where she had been a small boy who was put up those huge old chimneys as a sweep. She had actually died from this barbaric treatment. Since her regression she has had no more panic attacks and her breathing returned to normal, even during the regression.

Over the last twenty-five years I have cleared so many of these souls trapped in darkness that that is how I have come to my own conclusions on what ghosts are. It seems that most apparitions have died in some sort of trauma, whether it be fear, or any other form of negativity ranging from shame to even traumatic deaths. For example, a sound engineer I know had to go up to a disused airforce base to dismantle the radio equipment. He found staying there alone quite unnerving, as some nights he felt as though he were in the middle of a war: he would hear men running towards the aircraft hangers and he even heard their voices talking, yet saw nothing!

A few years ago, a man brought his thirty-five year old son to me for help. The son had suffered very deep depressions as a child, but they only occurred about once a year. Over the years the man and his wife watched the child and tried to put their finger on what set off this seemingly unaccountable gloom. It gradually dawned on them that these upsets occurred every year in early November around Remembrance Day, and as the child grew older the depressions became more severe and began to spread over longer periods. They finally heard a broadcast I did on radio and contacted me, and I put the son into regression.

> **He saw a life in the Second World War where he was in the army serving in France. He had been manning a small outpost and it had been taken by German soldiers. All his comrades had been killed and he heard the enemy approaching the room he was working in. Knowing he had no chance of escape, he did what most normal human beings would do and hid under a table. He was shot in his hiding place and died instantly, but in his mind he felt he had died a coward's death.**

This shame trapped him in that memory. When we discussed this later we both saw the fact that he had taken a small chance of escaping the inevitable and it had failed. He had not died a coward's death at all and seeing it from a calm, level situation the whole thing looked better. He was able to understand and begin to cope with the depressions that had for so long gripped his life.

It can be the same with some of our memories of growing up in this life, as we must all at some point in our lives have experienced something we felt ashamed of and hid in the recesses of our minds, only to find they remained there to torment us. Then when we looked again at them in later years, discovered we had been covering up something so piffling it was laughable. In some instances, these memories lurk in the darkness for so long that the person eventually has to go through extensive counselling to uncover and flush them out! Such memories can play a large part in that person losing faith in their self-worth.

Whilst dwelling on war memories I must mention another past life of someone who is quite well known, although in this case I won't be naming the person as he and I agreed it would be better to leave him anonymous in the circumstances. (In fact there are lots of celebrities that discovered past lives that for many different reasons we decided would be left untold.) This particular soul memory we agreed was too thought-provoking to leave out, but as it unfolds it will be self explanatory as to why it would be better not put a name to him. All I can tell you is that in this life he is very talented, highly respected and loved, as well he should be as he has worked so hard during this life to help others. In this life he was born to a Jewish family and brought up in the typical way of Judaism. In the past life that unfolded that day in my consulting room, his life was quite different.

> **He was a high-ranking Gestapo officer and helped bring about the deaths of hundreds of Jews. He died in some kind of bunker from a cause that we presumed must be of gas, as he died gasping for breath, but before he died he felt the pain of his deeds enormously, and died with such deep feelings of regret that his soul was trapped in that trauma and needed to be rescued.**

It took me a long while to get that aspect of his soul to see the light.

I have experienced many regressions with subjects who had lives connected in one way or another with the Second World War, perhaps because the circumstances of war create traumatic experiences which trap souls in darkness and prevent them from reaching the light. Many of them were concentration camp victims. Recently I was visited by a very prominent Jewish businessman who travels all over the world in the course of his work. However, he came to me to ask for help in ridding him of the fear he experienced every time he visited Germany. He is not, by nature, a nervous man – quite the reverse – as well as being a successful businessman he is a world champion yachtsman and holds many trophies for gliding. Every time he visited Germany, however, he felt as if he was looking over his shoulder in fear all the time. Matters came to a head when he was staying in lodgings with members of his team and found that his fear had reached such a state that he was too afraid even to go down the corridor in the night to the toilet. We found his last life hidden in his soul memory.

Once again, he was Jewish, but this time born in Germany. He was taken from a ghetto and imprisoned in Auschwitz concentration camp where he was forced to take the dead bodies from the gas chambers and throw them into huge trenches that he and the other prisoners had dug out. Eventually he was shot in the back by his captors and his body fell into the same trench.

On one trip to Germany, he had visited Auschwitz and the experience had brought forward such feelings of terror that he even feared he had been one of the aggressors. The regression therefore brought him immense relief and left him feeling much lighter. He has also been back to Germany since then and says he felt totally different about it and comfortable for the first time in years.

There have even been small children with memories of the Second World War. Years ago a lady writer called Mary Harrison came to seek my assistance. She was in the midst of writing a book, which she had formed the idea of writing whilst in hospital having a baby. She was talking to a Dr Fenwick, neurophysiologist at St Thomas's Hospital, London and Senior Lecturer at the Institute of Psychiatry, who mentioned scientific work which shows that the brain rhythms of babies in the last month before birth show changes which have been interpreted as periods during which they may be dreaming. This strongly suggests that the unborn child experiences dreams.

This caused Mary to wonder what the baby could be dreaming about, since it has not as yet had any of the experiences of life upon which earthly dreams are founded. She wondered whether the unborn baby be dreaming about a previous life in another realm. Mary also consulted Dr Arthur Guirdham, a psychiatrist from Bath well known for his work with children suffering from nightmares. He told her he is convinced that in many cases the bad dreams are due to traumatic experiences in previous lives. He felt this explanation can very often account for phobias and odd behaviour in children where the parents cannot trace any significant incident in their lives that could possibly be responsible. In many cases, neurotic behaviour can be traced back to a previous violent death, such as stabbing, drowning or a railway accident. These children show morbid fear of knives, water, trains and so on. Mary then decided that this seemed significant in the case for proof of past life, so she set up a tour of radio stations throughout England asking for parents to come forward who had any kind of experience of this from their offspring. The response was amazing, with some quite incredible proof, so this spawned her book *Life Before Birth* – a thoroughly good read and extremely well researched.

Amongst the small children that were brought forward was one boy who, from a very tender age, was obsessed with playing with toy planes, as many young boys are. However, this boy began to talk about the occasion when he had crashed his plane into a window.

As he grew older and his vocabulary and mastery of expression increased, he told this story in more and more detail, until finally his parents felt there was much more to this than a small child's imagination. Eventually, when he was playing with crayons and a colouring book, he drew unusual badges and insignia all over the page. The clarity of these drawings made his mother inspect them in detail, only to find she did not recognise any of these motifs, apart from one in the top corner of the page: it was a perfect German swastika inside a circle. When she questioned him about this he calmly informed her that these were the badges he wore on his uniform when he used to fly his plane.

Then to their further astonishment, on his fifth birthday he drew the cockpit of his plane. He remembered the exact position of all the controls and he explained to his bewildered parents the function of each lever, dial and gauge. He even knew the location of the button which he remembered having to press in order to release the bombs. After much questioning he came up with information that he could not possibly have known had he not been there, even to the minutest detail of there being sinks in his airbase rooms but no taps, only a pump.

All the information he gave later checked out. There are many similar, thought-provoking cases recounted in Mary Harrison's book, but in each case it was found that the child seemed to lose this far memory as he or she grew older and absorbed more learning and information from this life.

Mary Harrison came to me for regression to help her with her work on the book, and when regressed, went back to a life at the time of the battle of Culloden in Scotland in 1746. Her fiancé was killed in the battle and she never married. But that life had stayed with her to haunt her in her present life, as she used to have regular dreams of bloodied bandages wrapped around a tree and waving in the wind. When she went into her Culloden life, the bandaged tree was the first thing she saw! Even though she had come to me merely to research her book, not looking for a healing experience, she found that this recurring nightmare was then cleared. Another positive end to this tale is that she has now written a musical about the life she saw in my room, so I shall look forward to seeing the life unfold before me.

The recurring nightmare syndrome is very common and came up amongst some of our celebrities. I regressed the actress Lesley Dunlop because she had been having the same frightening dream since her early childhood. I had earlier regressed the man who played her screen husband in the television situation comedy *From May to December*, Anton Rodgers, although she did not know this. So it was a complete coincidence when she came to me on a professional appointment. I obviously do not tape such sittings, but was reminded of her regression whilst talking to her recently on the telephone. She gave me permission to include her experience and jogged my memory of what happened.

> Her nightmares had begun when she was about seven years old. She always saw herself in an old, oak-panelled room feeling very afraid. When I took her back she saw herself as a small girl aged seven and she walked into the same oak-lined room which seemed to be a library or study in her home. But instead of finding her father sitting at his desk, there was a German soldier in his place pointing a gun at her. We both found her reaction very strange. Instead of running away from this threat she said, 'I love you' but her affectionate greeting did her no good at all as he shot her dead!

Lesley tells me now she understands her fearful dream, the fear has gone. She was combining two parallel circumstances in a frightening way.

Whilst on the subject of fears, I must add that I met my husband, John Alkin, through his fears. We knew each other casually as we had friends in common, but he came to me one day and asked me if I could help him. He was an actor and he felt he had lost his confidence. You may remember him as Detective Constable Tom Daniels in *The Sweeney*. His life and marriage had broken down and he felt he was losing the plot. He was also suffering from recurrent nightmares. (I don't know whether I gave him another one by eventually marrying him!) He used to wake up frequently and feel that his guts where spilling out onto the bed. The regressions I did with him cleared the nightmares, re-established his belief in himself and helped him to regain his confidence.

In the past life that came forward, he had been a bit of a buccaneer. He lived on a farm, was very popular with the girls and very sure of himself and arrogant. He finally fell in love with one particular girl who went to a ball with someone else to make him jealous in the hope that he would take her seriously and settle down. Her plan backfired. His reaction was to down pints of ale at the local inn and then, in a drunken mood, go to the ball to confront his rival with a drawn sword. His rival – being considerably more sober and therefore more steady – drew his sword and ran him through. He lay there with his guts spilling out on to the ballroom floor and died in terrible guilt and humiliation. To his dreadful mortification, the last people he looked up at as he died were his girlfriend and his parents who all really loved him. His arrogance had done this terrible thing to the people he loved.

He has never had this nightmare again as the experience was cleared in the light. His other nightmare was when he would be woken up in the night with the feeling of falling. I again took him to his past to find a time he had been a sailor and had fallen from the crow's-nest in a rough sea to his death but not to the light. This nightmare has also never recurred, but interestingly he reads endless novels about ancient sea adventures and we also have a boat in this life. Old habits do die hard.

Another example of how trapped traumas can surface in dreams was with a lady who I regressed to find she had been a manservant to Anne Boleyn's family, and had gone with the servants when Anne had moved to the court of Henry VIII, and consequently shared Anne's sticky end. This particular person ended up hanged, drawn and quartered, a gruesome way of ending lives in that day and age. I took the part of her soul that belonged to that life to the light and she went home in a sort of daze. A couple of months later she faxed me to say that when she had been a girl at boarding school she had had a very vivid, recurring nightmare about awaiting an execution. She said she could hear the scaffolding being erected and she knew the outcome of the dream so well that she was able to wake herself up before the end and lay in bed reciting the Lord's prayer for protection. She told me that since that dream she had often woken in the night feeling terrified for no particular reason, but since that clearance of the soul in that one lifetime she has found her fear has gone.

The session I had with Nina Myskow explored two interesting lives reflecting an element of fear. I was pleased to add her to my list of subjects, not only because I enjoy her as a friend, but because she made her name as a critic and has never been afraid to say what she thinks. She is also highly intelligent and not easily fooled, so I was very glad that her regressions were not only a success but proved to be a healing power for her, too. Her first session was very short but potent so I will tell it in her words.

'I'm standing in front of an old wooden door. It's splintered and broken and has holes at the bottom where the rot has eaten it away. There's no handle, just a hole where it used to be. It's the door to a barn, a very dark barn. There is a bit of light, shafts of light, but it's mostly dark. It smells of hay, a thick smell.'

A fascinating part of regression is that the subject can often sense the smell quite clearly, and can also feel heat or gain other sensory impressions.

'There are no animals. I'm barefoot and wearing a brown sacking dress: it's ragged, dirty, rough, horrible and shapeless. I'm seven or eight years old and hate the barn. It's terrifying, dark and there's someone hiding there – a man. He's frightening because he's always trying to get me into the barn with him.'

I gently move her back in time to find out more about her life.

'I live in a simple cottage, which is all right, it's home. The kitchen is gloomy. I eat there with my older brother and our father. I don't like either of them. The man I fear works on a nearby farm; I see him often with pitchfork, cart and horse. I have to go into the barn. I don't like it at all, but I'm going in to hide from him, it's the only place to hide. It's dark, there is no hand rail – I'm falling down the wooden steps.'

At this point I had to intervene and clear this memory for her as she had obviously died from the fall and could see no more. She laughed about the sacking dress, as she is famous for wearing mainly pink in this life and loves beautiful clothes. She made the interesting observation that if she had imagined this strange life, she would definitely have chosen a better frock! She also hates the country and avoids farmland like the plague, and after seeing her last experience of farming, she realised why.

Many months later Nina rang me to say that up to that regression she had suffered very badly from hayfever, but since then had not had any symptoms at all. I felt that explained the overpowering smell of hay she sensed. It was not really hayfever but a bad memory trigger that had been causing her misery.

The second life was not a fun one either, but I have found in this work that the lives that most need to be cleared are always brought forward first, as they are the ones that need the healing touch. Again I'll leave the account of this one to Nina.

> 'I'm a seventeen year old girl standing in front of a bamboo door wearing a sarong. It's tropical and quite sort of jungley, with coconut palms, beach and sea. There's a bamboo hut there, and I'm all alone. There are lots of little houses on stilts over the water, like Polynesian huts. The place is lovely but there is something wrong with me. I ought to be happy but I'm not. All I know is I'm some sort of outcast and all by myself.'

I take her back further.

> 'I'm about ten years old now and in the same place. I'm with my mother. I hate her because she doesn't love me. She doesn't ever touch me and I think my father is dead.'

I take her back to her father's death.

'I'm very little, a girl of about five. My father died because of me. I was swimming when I had been told I shouldn't and he had to help me. It's all my fault that he died and that's why my mother never touches me.'

We go to the last memory of this life.

'I'm in a dugout boat. I'm out at sea and the sea is very turbulent. There's a storm and it's dark. Suddenly I'm not in the water any more . . .'

At that point she drowned and we both felt she had given up on life and gone out to sea to try to join her father.

There are many kinds of fear that show themselves in different illnesses. Agoraphobia is one very common example. I must stress again, of course, that many cases of such phobias are not started in past lives, but started by events in childhood in this life. However, two cases I dealt with recently are useful examples of those that are triggered by earlier experiences.

One lady telephoned me in a terrible state. She was afraid of leaving the house at all, and if she did manage to summon the courage to go out, she got herself into the most dreadful state of panic. Not surprisingly, she didn't manage to turn up for her first two appointments. When she finally did make it and was shown into the waiting room, there was someone waiting to collect the client who was with me. The poor woman almost broke into hysteria and turned a strange purplish colour, so my assistant had to invite her to wait in her office and managed to keep her there for fifteen minutes until I started her treatment.

During the first session, I concentrated on giving her healing to calm her down and help me get to know more about her. Once that had been achieved, I felt that regression would help, so we organised a return visit the following week. She made her next appointment without any problem, and said that her feeling of calm had lasted most of the week, giving her a rest from her panic and allowing some strength to return.

When I put her into regression she described a life as a woman in what appeared to be England, where she lived quite an uneventful life. However, when she recalled her death, she found that she was in a coffin and was scratching and screaming to get out. She had been mistaken for dead and buried alive.

Such a traumatic end to a life takes patience and care to clear. I actually had to hold her physically to help her regain her calm, which is very unusual. Although her nature remains highly strung, she is now a different person: she goes out, drives her car, and she is even writing a book.

Fears such as agoraphobia can strike quite suddenly. One client had quite a normal life until two years before he sought my help. He had been crossing a road when he was suddenly gripped by total fear and panic. From that moment on he became a prisoner to this fear and going out had become a nightmare.

When we looked at his past he was shown a life in the English countryside, which, judging by the period, I felt was the life immediately before his present one. It was when cars were a rare and unexpected sight, especially in the countryside. He had crossed his normally deserted lane to go to a post box, when a car came round the bend and as he was blinded by the car's headlights he stumbled into the vehicle and was instantly killed.

After we cleared this memory away, he told me that when he had had his first panic attack he had been looking up a dark road and the headlights of a bus had been the last thing he saw before he began to shake! The experience had been so similar to the one in his earlier life, that it had triggered the memory which otherwise might have remained dormant.

Often these soul memories can be triggered by a person meeting again in this life someone who had been with them in a previous one. A girl came to me who had been a very sporting person – hang-gliding and abseiling were some of her many pastimes, and she certainly had no fear of heights. Then she met her present husband and after they married she developed an irrational terror of heights.

When she saw her past life, she saw a time when she had fallen in love with a boy who lived in a modest terraced house, similar to her own, in the next street. She married her love, but as finances were very tight they had to live with his mother whom she did not get on with at all. She had a baby and after the birth fell into deep depression that she could not shake. Finally one day she walked calmly upstairs and threw herself from the highest window, killing herself on the pavement below.

After the regression, the woman lost her new-found fear of heights. It seemed that she had met again the boy she had married in her past life, a marriage that had caused such misery. This time she was extremely happily married and we felt she had returned to get her relationship right this time.

Feelings of guilt can also have their source in past, rather than present, lives. One normally outgoing and sunny lady came to me because she had recently become gloomy and oppressed, feeling a sense of guilt and always believing that everything that went wrong was her fault. She could not think of anything that had triggered these depressive feelings.

I regressed her to a life in Italy hundreds of years

earlier with her very strict Catholic family. She had fallen head over heels in love with a boy whom her father felt was totally unsuitable, so the family had sent her to a convent in Spain for the rest of her life. Although she did not have the calling to be a nun, she eventually settled to her enforced way of living and spent many hours writing poetry, but also became very religious and God-fearing and achieved a kind of happiness in her work for God. Then one day the convent was overrun by soldiers who pillaged and destroyed the convent, raping any desperate women who crossed their paths. She was raped, strangled and thrown down a well shaft.

What happened next quite startled me as – right in front of me in this life – she fell to her knees and wept hysterically. I finally comforted her and coaxed her to the light, but only after she confessed that she had enjoyed her first sexual encounter and felt the guilt so powerfully that she became trapped in her dark, well grave. Later as we discussed the experience we realised that the memory had been triggered when she had taken her daughter to enrol in a school in a convent with nuns as teachers.

Another client that I feel falls into the right category for this chapter had what was not exactly a fear but a feeling of unease accompanied by pains. This particular girl is under my guidance developing as a healer. Just before this regression, something had occurred in her life that she knew was a test of her faith. She had developed an illness that she knew would only go by her having the strength of faith to make it go. When my pupils are under development they generally come, at the right time, to need a clearance. This means that a life in the past is brought forward so strongly that every time they meditate they feel actual physical discomfort. This client was experiencing pains in her legs and abdomen, so we organised a regression so that I could bring this life forward.

The life that came showed her in a cave wearing coarse, sacking clothing. I thought at first I had got my first cave man, but she could see no more so I took her back to when she was a child to find she was a young boy happily living in a close family unit, when suddenly her parents were killed in an accident. The boy was sent to a boarding school and adjusted well until he left to start work. He then found he felt utterly alone and could not face the life so he joined a monastery and became a monk. At first all was very well, but he was different from the other monks, for they were leading that life because of their faith whereas he had no faith at all. In spite of all the other monks for company he still felt entirely alone. He also had the added discomfort of having normal male sexual desires. He finally went to a cave where he beat himself with a boulder around his genital and abdomen area. He died from his wounds.

I did not quite clarify whether he meant to kill himself or just rid himself of his sexual desires, as I did not want to hold him there in his pain.

After the session we discussed what we had just witnessed and she now realises that this past life is parallel to where she is up to in this life. Her faith in the light is now complete, but the experience showed that she also has to have absolute faith in herself for the light to flow through her as a clear channel for the healing power. So she now realises that her test of faith is not with the light, or God, but in herself to be a good worker. I felt this example was a slightly gory one, but very expressive.

And whilst on the subject of fear brought about by guilt, I'll end with a regression with a man who is very prominent in his field of work. He came to me because he felt he had lost his way in life. This was extremely painful for him as he was a teacher and felt he no longer had authority.

His session brought him forward as a young girl who lived with her parents but was very unhappy because her father would often beat her and her mother. Eventually, her life was unbearable. At the height of one attack, she grabbed a carving knife and stabbed her father in the stomach. In her fear and panic she could not face up to what she believed she had done, so she ran away and drowned herself in a nearby lake.

When we took her to the light, we discovered by looking back that she had not killed him at all, merely wounded him. Later we analysed the whole thing and realised that the school he had seen in his regression had been almost identical to one he was sent to about the time his trouble began.

These examples clearly show a pattern. Just as a traumatic memory in this life can be suppressed and later affect the personality, traumatic events in a past life can do the same. Encountering an experience which parallels something in a previous life can trigger that soul memory and mean that a person is almost living in the past. Through regression these memories can be unearthed, and the darkness cleared.

I hope that the changes in attitude towards regressional therapy – and other complementary treatments – will continue to change so that (in my lifetime, I hope) regression will become a normally accepted therapy. If we look back in history to the tribal patterns that were so natural for humans for so long, we can see that we have moved away from that. They had all manner of help within their own clan – the close family, the counsellor, the seer, the healer – many of whom used natural 'magic' such as crystals and colour healing. Just as we have lost our old-style families, we have also lost many of our gifts and arts. But I think we are becoming more open-minded again and I trust that the wheel is turning.

❖

Talents from the Past

I n many of the past lives I have brought forward I have found that, when the time is right, something that one has learned or accomplished in the past is brought into the present memory. That way the accomplishment is strengthened and re-established to be used again in this lifetime. This has happened to me at very valuable times and to great effect, so it came as no surprise when I found talents from the past shown to us in the celebrities I encountered, amongst them Lynsey de Paul, Wayne Sleep, Billie Jean King and Elton John.

The singer and composer Lynsey De Paul is a very tiny lady, although large in talent. In addition to her musical successes, such as her hits with *Colour Me* and *Rock Bottom*, she has also written a book on self-defence which proves that even someone as small as herself can manage a huge bully. Hers was a very interesting case, as three lives were brought forward. The first was totally uneventful, but during the second she began her affair with the keyboard, which was carried on into her third life, this time becoming professional as, of course, she has done in this life. I liked the fact that the music seemed to build towards this life, and I also felt that her seeing the uneventful life first knocked the cynics' eye view of thinking that celebrities only see what they want to see. To show this point I'll print all three of her memories in the order in which she saw them.

'I can see a girl – it could be me. I think it's the fifteenth century. She's got her hair pulled back and her whole head, apart from the front of her hair, is under this little, white cotton bonnet thing; it's not a hat. It covers the back of the head and then there's a stiff frill of cotton. I think she's a servant in a house. She's wearing a white apron over a dark maroon skirt with petticoats under and a little dark top. It's all very plain, she's definitely not someone of any standing. She's between seventeen and twenty. The house is not huge, it's not a Duke of Westminster-type place, but it's a good home and belongs to someone of some standing in the community.

'She was about thirteen when she first came to work at this house. She had been brought up locally, without education, by hard-working folk. The father had some sort of trade but I don't know exactly what, and the mother did odd jobs to help out but didn't really work apart from coping with the home and children. She was sent off early into service because they didn't want to pay for her keep. She was sent off as soon as she was old enough to earn her own living.

'She sleeps in an extremely bare room that has a fireplace. There are small, leaded windows, plain bed and plain floorboards, very grey altogether. She's not unhappy; she doesn't even think of it. She cleans out the fireplaces and does all the menial jobs, and eats her meals with the rest of the staff in a kitchen room. She doesn't question anything, she just accepts it all, glad to be clothed and fed and looked after. She's not stupid, just naive and simple. Because she stays in the same position and works hard, she gains more trust as the years go by. She never goes out socially but is quite content. By the time she's in her forties, she is running part of the kitchen – that's her life. At fifty she has become frail and can't do too much work. The whole of her working life has been spent in this same house and she dies in her little bed . . . a totally uneventful life . . . it was really wasted.'

I could feel Lynsey's disappointment at what she had just seen, so guided her straight on into the next memory to erase the feeling.

'I'm looking at something carved in wood and I'm very, very small, I'm just about walking. I'm wearing white and in someone's bedroom; there's lots and lots of carved wood, sort of Jacobean. I can't tell whether I'm a boy or a girl.'

I guide her on to the age of ten.

'I still can't tell! I'm either a girl or a very feminine boy. I think it's when they had a custom of dressing little boys the same way as girls. Yes, I'm a boy. I'm wearing laces and velvets and have long ringlets.

'When I'm grown up I'm wearing Mozart-type clothes and sitting in front of a keyboard. It's a harpsichord, with two tiers with black notes and white notes, the reverse of a piano. I play by ear but I don't compose. I'm the son of a quite well-to-do family, so I don't have to rush out to work early in life. My father exports textiles. He deals in cloth and wears a lovely long, dark wig with ringlets. He's very dominant and I can't even see my mother.

'By the time I'm thirty I'm married and live in the same house with my parents. There's one child just been born and another a few years old. I'm now in the same business as my father. I see by looking at the huge family bible that it's written in Flemish. I only play the harpsichord as a hobby now. My life has just followed the order of things.

'By fifty my father is dead and I run the whole household. There are still only two children; there was a third but it died. The marriage is fine. It's very cordial, although it's never been very passionate on my part. I die in my late sixties of the gout, basically the body just stopped working properly.'

I know it has sometimes confused people who have read some of the regressions as to how the subjects know particular facts. In this case, for example, that she had two children but there had been a third who died. This is quite a common thing, as when the sitter is reliving the life their mind just knows certain things. Another example was that Ian Lavender knew he was a fish merchant, although I had not taken him to where he worked. It was simply something that came into his mind while in the past memory.

The third life we went on to see was quite unusual because Lynsey had relived it once before. I have had clients that have gone back to the same life again, but generally it was because there was something in the life that still needed to be understood. I can only presume that this life is so close to her still that she draws upon it easily. Here is what she saw and what she learnt about this life during her regressions.

'I'm seeing the same life very clearly that I had before when I was regressed by Dr Larive (Doctor of Metaphysics). It's about 1720 and I'm a boy living just outside Hamburg. It's not a very poor family.

I'm wearing the style of the day, not dissimilar in fashion to the last life I saw, as it appears to be quite soon afterwards. It's such a strong memory.'

Lynsey went on to describe what she saw and what she learnt about the same life from the previous regression.

'As a young boy I showed a tremendous aptitude for music and was sent by my parents to study in Hamburg. I was sort of 'gopher' cum apprentice for the composers of that time. They weren't very well known composers; there were loads of composers then whose work never survived them. I started out working for these sort of people. I can see the room I worked in: it was a small room with a table and candle on it, a chair and simple bed. I was set to copy out their manuscripts. The composer would write something and I would have to painstakingly write it out for them beautifully, a sort of calligraphy of music. I was apprenticed to learn composition, play the harpsichord and be a student of this person. I didn't earn much but I just about got by. I was very happy as it was leading to good things and meant I wouldn't have to be a peasant.

'Eventually I ended up working and living in the palace in Hamburg. It was a huge and magnificent place. The room where I ate my meals was lovely but wasn't nearly as wonderful as the dining hall where the owners ate. The servants were answerable to me, but I was answerable to the top echelon. They had very big wigs and lacy cuffs and I had a wig that had only two rolls on it and no lace on the cuffs. The big wigs really were the big wigs. I worked my way up there to become the resident musical director of that court, and if a maestro was coming to do a concert, they would send the scores on ahead with their servants and I would re-copy them, rehearse the orchestra from the harpsichord and then when the maestro came everything would be ready for him to just go and do his performance and I would step back for him. There was no accolade at all.

'The most poignant memory is of my snuff-taking habit. One always kept snuff in the left-hand pocket, then took it out in the left hand and flipped the lid open and took a pinch and put it on the back of the hand to sniff it up. Those with no lace were able to use the back of the hand, whereas if you had the lacy cuffs you couldn't put it on the back of the hand, so you would just take a pinch of snuff. I had a wonderful filigree snuff box measuring about two inches by one and a half inches, with a door that opened in it rather than the whole edge opening up, and it flicked up broadside not longside. There was a tremendous hierarchy involved in taking snuff because it was very expensive. It was social snobbery. I don't know whether I actually enjoyed it, but it did clear the sinuses.

'I never married. There was a woman once, who was more of a friend than anything else, but I was attracted to both men and women, although I paid more attention to my career than to romance. I feel I was dedicated to my music and the court because of my low beginnings. It was my utter life: I loved the music and was a very competent musician. I wasn't a great composer, just competent, and a good resident musical director. I didn't hold any great sway, like I was anything of tremendous importance within the palace, but I held a position of rank. I lived in a wing of the palace where all the servants lived. My room was of oak but it was a very light oak; I suppose it went black over the years! It was a nice room with a lovely four-poster bed, but it had no top or canopy on it, just four posts going up to nothing. There was a desk and chair and a cupboard built into the wall.

'I lived to a very ripe old age, mid-seventies, and died in my bed mainly due to old age. I felt very proud of myself because I had upheld my honour and been dedicated to my career and had approval from great people of that time and also royalty. I felt I achieved a tremendous amount.'

Lynsey talked later about how she felt about the regressions.

'Those two first lives were not like me at all now because I question everything and I'm here not to follow convention and rules and not to be encumbered by other people but to make life as much of an adventure as possible. If there's something I think I'd like to do, I do it. I'm not daunted by anything. It worried me being a man and being bisexual, because in this life I'm not like that at all. Mind you I feel he did nothing much at all about his sexuality; he was all career.

'I felt that the second life prepared me, or planted the seed, for my music, but the last life is the most interesting. In this life, I have Dutch, German and Austrian heritage, and I feel I've brought the talent of piano playing through into this life with me, as I began playing at the age of four, and was able to pick out melodies before I was big enough even to span an octave. I feel it is a talent that has stayed with me. The strange thing is I was brought up with Beethoven and Tchaikovsky because my father didn't like Bach, but when I was eventually introduced to Bach by my music mistress at The Royal Academy, it was like I hadn't drunk for a long time and couldn't stop drinking. I didn't want to play anything else and I played as fast as I could. It felt like remembering rather than learning. When I was taught German at school (I did German for an A level) I spoke it so quickly, it was bizarre. Aristotle said, "All learning is just the soul remembering," and in this case I feel he's right.'

I found it interesting to note Lynsey's observations about the light oak panelling in one of the rooms she saw, and her remark that the oak must blacken over the years. I went to Lynsey's home to do this session and it is a most wonderful, old place that is panelled throughout in oak. I feel it is significant that she saw the oak as it would have been all those years ago and not, as one might expect, as she sees it every day of her present life.

Wayne Sleep was another celebrity who saw success in a musical career, but that time not in dancing, as in his present life.

'I'm inside a very light room with green carpets. I'm facing an old leather chair, like a Chesterton-type chair. There's not much else in the room. It has white walls and a large window that looks out on to a lawn.

'I'm wearing brown suede shoes, the old-fashioned Oxford type with thick woollen socks and jodhpurs, gaiters, shirt and waistcoat. My hair is brown and longish in style. I'm carrying a stick in my hand. I've just returned from a walk. It's one of those sticks you sit on, a shooting stick. I'm about fifty-five years of age. I look like a country gentleman.

'My house is in a village and it looks like a Victorian-style cottage on a lane with other cottages. Inside there's a lady in the kitchen in a long black dress with an apron over the top and a mob cap on her head; she's our maid. She's standing by a very long wooden table.

'It's night-time now and I'm having dinner at a

very shiny dining table with lots of silver laid out on it; it's beside a shiny elegant fireplace. I'm sitting to one side of the table and opposite me is a lady with long black hair and a dress down to the ground. I'm not sure if it's my wife.'

I take him to see the contents of the bedroom to find out, and we establish that his wardrobe has her clothes in it, too. It's a very small, wallpapered bedroom and has a small bed. We go back to when he was thirty.

'I'm at work. I'm the village vicar in the Anglican church there. It's a small church with a square tower and is built entirely of stone. It's surrounded by fields. Inside the walls are painted white to half way up. It's a Sunday and I'm in the pulpit and I'm taking the Holy Communion service. I'm very contented in my work and my home life. We have no children but we are happy.'

We go back to when he was a boy.

'I'm twelve years old and running through the street with a hoop, propelling it with a stick. I've got a really snotty nose and I'm very dirty.'

I was amused to note that Wayne seemed horrified at this!

'I decided I wanted to be a priest when I was at school. I thought it would be a good way of escape.'

I ask what he wanted to escape from.

'From poverty. At the very end of this life I'm in bed dying quietly. I feel I discovered peace in this life.'

Wayne said at the end of all his memories that he felt the religious life had had an effect on his present life, as when he was younger he was very involved with the Church, in particular with the Church Army. He was in the choir and at church all day sometimes. In fact when he was ten he had made his mind up to be a priest, but then he won a scholarship to The Royal Ballet School and his religious ambitions were pushed into the background. He still feels an affinity with God because, as he says, he was 'born like that', and feels God is with him all the time.

I have a personal understanding of that, because it fits in with how I have been influenced by my past life as a nun. Many times in my life have been difficult and I have felt low, and always at those times I thought about becoming a nun. Even as a child when I didn't get my way at home, I would tell myself I would leave and become a nun. I suppose if you have ever had a life that gave you security, it will always be an attraction in times of stress.

Throughout the years of my healing work, I have often been consulted by nuns, priests and even monks. Mostly they have come for healing, but others have come to discuss the healing process and to discover what beliefs I hold. I even knew a nun who used to ring me on a regular basis. I never knew her name or where she rang from, but she was full of questions and I like to think I helped her with her struggle within herself. Twice I have been visited by men of the cloth whom I have been certain have lived a secure past life in the Church and really should not have followed the same path in this lifetime. One of those concerned eventually left his ministry and ended up running a night club! He is still a religious man but feels he is more effective in offering support to young people in his new vocation.

A hairdresser friend of mine, who has many famous clients, saw a life in regression when he became the Pope. But on his death, when he was laid in state in his coffin with people filing past him, I had great trouble getting him to the light as even though he had reached such heights in his chosen life, he didn't actually believe in God at all and was afraid to leave for what he felt was oblivion. Wayne, on the other hand, I felt had become a good vicar. His next life seemed out of sequence somehow, and I felt should have preceded the vicar but, as I have said, I have no control over how the past lives push themselves forward. This is how Wayne described this life.

> 'I'm looking at a gypsy camp on the moors. It's freezing and they are all camped around a fire. I'm a boy in rags. I live under the steps of my father's caravan. It's very hard. My father is a big man and mother is very drawn-looking with a tired face. The caravan is all wooden like a true Romany gypsy van but not at all ornate. There's a horse and it stinks; there are more horses and they all stink. It's a small camp with only about five vans.'

We move on to the age of twenty.

> 'I'm still living the same kind of life. I feel we are on the Devon moors. I reach the age of thirty with not much change, except I now have a wife and children. I'm not sure if I am actually married to her, though. Life is hard and I'm always angry and tired; always, since the first memory, I've felt tired. I make a rough living selling horses.'

We move on to the end of this drab life.

> 'I'm forty-five now and I'm dying of pneumonia. I'm sweating and shivering in the small, cold van. I feel this life wasn't worth living, except for one thing – I did learn to love, I've learnt to love my wife and children. I didn't at first, not for a long

time, but I learnt to love – it was hard to do.'

Wayne's fourth regression seems to have begun his musical career. Here it is as it came through.

'I'm standing by a wide, curved staircase with iron banisters curving upwards. The house is very grand with many chandeliers and lots of light; it catches light from all angles. The walls are covered in lovely paintings of horsey scenes and portraits, and the whole place is surrounded by lovely grounds. I'm wearing a long, silk dressing gown and matching hat with tassels. Beneath that there's a shirt and bow tie. I'm getting ready to receive guests. I put on a dinner suit. My hair is grey; I guess I'm about fifty years old. My party guests are quite grand: there's a general and many other army types amongst them.'

We go back to the age of thirty.

'I'm playing a violin in the study to a private gathering of people, an intimate kind of concert.'

I manage to get him even further back.

'I'm about twelve. I've got lovely, gold, curly locks and am dressed in black velvet with a big white collar. I'm in a much different house: it's darker, it's a middle class house with steps leading up to the front door. I'm living with my grandmother. My mother died when I was about three years old and my father went away to sea and died there. I was brought up by my grandmother. She's quite posh but she's very old and this tended to suppress me.
'I was quite young when I first went to work

and I worked in the shipyard in charge of making inventories of nautical things. I work in the office and on the big ships. I'm seeing myself making an inventory of the cargo on a big steamer with smoke billowing out of yellowish funnels.'

We go forward a little in time.

'I've left my job to take up playing professional violin. I began playing the violin when I was sixteen. It was on the sideboard all the time I was a child and the case was always open; it was like a presentation showcase thing. I wasn't interested in any kind of other work, I just wanted to play the violin. I had always been fascinated by it.

'I'm playing professionally now in a hall, like a village hall. I'm hearing the music now but it's not classical music as I expected, I'm hearing an Irish jig. The people are dancing, they're dancing up a storm – I'm playing fiddle music! I think it's Ireland; the music is very fast, they love it. The people are in old costumes, old dresses, some quite well-to-do, a very mixed gathering. It's a harvest do or something.'

We go to see the height of his career, which Wayne finds astonishing.

'I'm playing for royalty! It's Victorian. It's a huge concert. I'm not the only artiste, there are lots more. It's some kind of royal gala. It looks like the Albert Hall; it really seems to be the Albert Hall.

'At the end of my life I'm at sea. I think I'm on tour, and there's a huge storm. I'm in the water grasping at pieces of wood. It's gone dark.'

Wayne said later how amazed he was that he actually

heard the fiddler playing. He couldn't say whether drowning had made him afraid of sailing because he has never sailed, but he added perhaps that's why he'd never fancied it. He felt he had brought some of his tastes for the classical from that life, and thought that the violinist was very close to how he is in this life. As he took his leave a while later he was still exclaiming with amazement that he actually heard the violin playing, just as though he had been there in person.

Another fascinating celebrity I regressed was the world champion American tennis player, Billie Jean King, who has more recently concentrated on coaching another world champion, Martina Navratilova, to her record-breaking Wimbledon championship that beat Billie's own record. A few years ago we spent Christmas together in Acapulco in Mexico, as we were both staying in a villa there as guests of our mutual friend Elton John. She's such a powerful woman that I wasn't at all surprised when, exploring her far memory, we discovered that she, too, fitted into the category of being well known in a former life. In fact, we brought forward four lives and in most of them she was a very successful person. I'll leave you to read it in Billie's own words.

'I'm seeing a naked, white beach. It seems like the west side of Florida; it's the Everglades. I'm sleeping in the open under the stars. I'm an American Indian of the Seminole tribe. My feet are very worn and tanned dark brown and I always walk barefoot. They're a woman's feet. I'm wearing very colourful clothes with beads and strong colours of turquoise and reds. I'm about twenty years old and seem to have distanced myself from my family and friends and the rest of the tribe.

'Ten years later I'm still in the same place, in similar clothes, standing over a huge pot, cooking a meal. I'm in front of what looks like a tepee. It's the same tribal situation and I'm not really delighted at all.

'Yet another ten years later and I feel I'm stuck with the tribe. That's the deal. There's no fulfilment, no contentment, all there is to do is chores. My brain is going a mile a minute. If only I could be free. The men are not free. No one is free. We are here because we have to be, we have been pushed here by others.'

We were left with the strange power of desolation and sadness that made the room feel heavy, so I took her straight on to the next memory.

'This time I'm in a city. It's Russia. I'm wearing a tutu – I'm a ballerina, dancing and loving every minute of it, the music, the dance. I'm about eighteen years old and at training school. I'm happy, I feel like I can fly.

'Seven years on I'm a star, the best! It's cold but it doesn't bother me. It seems to be Leningrad in the 1800s.

'Ten years later I'm in my late thirties. I'm still there but I'm teaching now. I love helping the other people. I'm still to be found dancing once in a while and work at the barre every day. It's still exciting to get up in a morning, but the beds are so short! I'm alone but happy.

'Ten years on again, I'm into my late forties. I'm travelling and still teaching, but wanting more and more to know what the rest of the world is about.

'I'm still travelling five years further on, but I'm no longer happy. I have learned more about the Western world and know that it is far better than our way. I got my wish to learn more of the world by travelling but sadly it has only brought me total discontentment.'

As in the first life she was in, she didn't really see the end of it but knew she had died shortly after the disillusionment set in, and seemed to see her next life almost immediately.

'It's the Middle East. I'm a man – I'm a soldier. I'm not completely sure what my position is, but I feel I'm an officer in my early twenties. Could it be Charlemagne's time?

'By the time I reach thirty I'm an old man, as people die much younger in these times. I'm very happy at how my life has gone, though, I'm contented and I feel I can live happily with myself. I feel I did my duty and that I was one of the lucky ones to have reached such an old age. I've lived through the Crusades. I'm still in uniform, it's sort of a Ben Hur-style of garment.

'I feel I live on to almost forty years old and I can see myself passing peacefully.'

She then surprised me by almost taking herself on to the next life, as I was about to close the session, being quite pleased with what we had already achieved. So we'll keep up with her pace and carry on.

'I'm in Europe. My whole life is music. I'm a pianist aged about thirty-five and I'm a man. I practise the piano for about six to eight hours every day. It doesn't bother me, I'm very happy. I'm a professional and play for small, intimate audiences and sometimes in people's homes. I have even played for royalty. I later get to play at very large venues accompanied by an orchestra. At the height of my career I'm in Vienna playing for a very large audience for that time.'

Billie then went into the light and it was all over. Once

more she didn't see the death. In fact she never really spoke much of the style or buildings, but she was so deeply into the emotion and experience of the whole session that I didn't interject and break the spell. I found it interesting that she had been a pianist, as she adores Elton John and his talent. They seem to have so much in common, and she never misses his shows when she is able to get there. She has often coached Elton with his tennis playing – he really takes his game seriously – so they have mutual admiration. Perhaps he will return next time to become a world champion player!

Billie's comments on these past glimpses appear to back up my theory. She is in this lifetime a very good dancer and has surprised many of her friends in the tennis world by giving impromptu performances at many of the end-of-tournament parties. She told me she still loves performing, as in her chosen profession, and loves shaping time and space to bring the best she can possibly bring to everything she involves herself in. She is an ardent fan of the ballet and of piano concerts. She is known for her ready will to fight for people's freedom of choice. She admires justice and is persistent and loyal to many needy causes.

The teaching element has really carried forward from past to present life, as in addition to coaching that other great champion, Martina Navratilova, she spends a great deal of time coaching young people with potential but not the funds to take extra lessons, people who would normally never get the chance to be trained, particularly by such an expert. At present her whole life is dedicated to the advancement of the talent she discovers, as she loves teaching and creating opportunities for others. Her perseverance in reaching the top in her chosen path has certainly carried through for us all to see and I am sure there will be many champions to come who will owe it all to Billie Jean King.

Just after this session, Billie had to rush off to catch a plane, but she said the whole thing had made her feel at peace with the world and very calm. She rang later and said the feeling had lasted throughout her journey and into the next few days. She did remark at the time that it would be a great help to tennis players to be put into this state of calm before their matches. After she left my room she rushed round the villa to find Elton John and suggested that he should experience the same thing, as she felt it would be good for him. I had previously asked Elton myself to sit for me for this book, but he refused because he was sure that this was his first and last time here! After Billie spoke to him, he told me he would like to be regressed if I so wished. So thanks to Billie Jean I made the discovery that Elton, too, had a musical past. We later found out that not only was he wrong in thinking he hadn't had one past life, but we discovered three of them. Here's what Elton saw.

'I'm greeted in a dark, sombre hallway by a small shaggy dog. It's a dark, stone house with a very big hall. The stone work is very old, the place is cold and dreary. I really don't like it here at all.

'The dining room has a long wooden table, a fireplace, and the walls are all stone. This room is very large and there are two or three people in the room. I can't make them out very well but they're wearing very old clothes, velvets, it looks like pre-Elizabethan. The woman is wearing a long dress. It's not a poor house, it's very big but there are no ornaments of any kind. I'm now sitting in the centre, at the side of the dining table. There's a man at the head of the table – I think he's my father – and another man on my left and the woman is sitting opposite me and I feel she's my mother. We are being served food by two women wearing aprons.

'I can't see the stairs but I'm now in the upper part of the house in a small bedroom with a fireplace and window, again very bare. There's a bed and a table with a candle on it. I'm wearing long, skin boots on my small feet, and a long shirt. I'm a boy of about eight years old. It's a cold, lonely life, and I die very young, there are no more memories past this point.'

I took Elton away from this young death and hoped, as I put him into his second memory, that it would be more comfortable. I was not to be disappointed.

'I'm standing in a garden looking at a beautiful French château surrounded by fields. It's my house. I enter through a magnificent wooden door with gold trim. It's an ornate house with gold leaf all over the place. I take hold of the door handle with a gloved hand. I'm a twenty-eight year old man, very finely dressed, rather like a cavalier, with long, curly hair, a large hat and belt with buckle and sword. The house is lavish and crammed full of beautiful things. There are paintings of family: my mother and father and a separate one of me. The hallway is light, very light, it's full of beauty and I'm obviously wealthy. The gardens are laid out in symmetrical detail. It's a typical French château.

'There's a long dining table, (not nearly as long as the first one I saw, though). It seats about sixteen people on gold chairs. I can't see anyone else, I seem to be eating alone. I'm being served by a young footman who brings me wine and a bird, a game bird.

'Now I'm sitting in a beautiful, beautiful room with a piano. I'm alone and sitting at the piano playing. I'm not writing or reading music; I know it's my own composition.

'I socialise a lot in Paris. I see myself eating a meal in a restaurant. There are six people including myself, all wearing similar clothing, late eighteenth century, fine and ornate, and we are all wearing wigs. We are just six men at the table, no ladies, though there are ladies in the restaurant. We are talking and laughing and being very loud.

'I'm now seeing myself in my early forties. I'm in Venice and I'm very ill. I'm looking out across the bay to the other side of Venice and I know I'm gravely ill. This is the hour before my death. There's a priest by my bed.'

This memory had been so parallel to his present life that I thought we would end there, but he immediately saw the next one.

'All I can see is mud – I'm a soldier in khaki and am wearing a tin hat. I'm covered in mud. I'm in the trenches and it's the First World War.'

We move on to the next day.

'We're marching along a road and I'm absolutely exhausted. We get to a bombed out house and we all flop down inside to rest. It's France.'

We go forward one year.

'I'm in hospital. I've been injured, there's shrapnel in my leg and I'm here to have it taken out. My wife's at the bedside. She's a small, dark-haired woman, she's only about twenty-three. The war is over for me now.'

We go forward about twenty years.

'I'm a bus driver in London. It seems to be the

early forties. I'm living in the same small, terraced house that I was born and brought up in. The wife and I live with my parents, we have no children.'

We go to the end of this life.

'I'm aged about forty now. I'm driving the bus. I've lost control and it crashes. Everything's gone dark.'

Just before we closed this session he saw a brief life as a boy on a farm who had died very young, rather like the first one he had seen. But that night, in his dreams, he heard a tune so vividly that it woke him up. It excited him so much that he tried to find someone else awake to tell, but we were all asleep so he returned to his bed, only to dream again and hear the same melody as before. When he told me next morning I suggested that he write it down, but he said he could clearly recall it still. He has since added words to this tune and it is on his album 'Sleeping with the Past' which also features the number *Healing Hands*.

It seems too much of a coincidence to have such an experience just after seeing his past life as a composer. When discussing it later he said he saw he was very much like he is now only much more wealthy! He has always been attracted to France – especially Paris – and feels right when he's there, and particularly loves the special aroma there that always seems to move him. He speaks excellent French and until recently had a second home there. There is no need to point out the extreme similarity to the French life and how he has lived since he became famous. In fact, his home is filled with beautiful objects once more. He still loves to dine in the best restaurants surrounded by his friends. The flamboyance of his dress, and the memorable concert in Sydney when he sported a powdered wig, look very like his previous incarnation. Also he threw a fancy dress birthday party one year and I called in at his house on my way to the event to find him looking just like the man we saw on the day in Mexico!

He laughed heartily about the bus driver and said he'd never hear the end of it from his friends. He doesn't know whether he has an aversion to travelling on buses as he owns a fleet of cars ... but he never drives, he has a driver.

Elton's feelings for France reminded me of when I regressed John Lennon's first wife, Cynthia. She had a life in France as a priest. At one point she saw herself standing in the pulpit but there was no congregation. I had forgotten the details, as it was a long time ago, but I bumped into her recently and she reminded me. She said that it had had a profound effect on her and she had renewed her love for France and now has a permanent base there.

I had also at that time regressed Ringo Starr's first wife Maureen, who tragically died last year and is missed by all of us. At the end of her regression she went into the light and was very emotional when she was reunited with one of her closest relatives; I think it was her mother. At least we know that Maureen is now with that loved one!

I could not think of writing this chapter on talents that have grown like love over many lifetimes, without adding someone who was much loved and sadly missed, Tommy Nutter, the Savile Row tailor, whose clients included Mick and Bianca Jagger, Eric Clapton, Tim Rice and, of course, The Beatles (three of whom wore his suits on the famous *Abbey Road* cover). He also did Jack Nicholson's wonderful wardrobe for the film *Batman*. Unfortunately he died a short while ago, but a year before his death I had gone along to his apartment in Mayfair and regressed him. As a tribute to him I would like to include that session. He had hoped, before his untimely death, to distribute an exclusive range of men's perfumes and toiletries of his own, and was researching the project when I last saw him. I didn't say at the time, but I felt that his ambition for that enterprise was rather like my desire to be a nun; the time to make it happen had already passed. Anyway, here is the soul memory of Tommy Nutter (1943-1992).

'I'm seeing wrought-iron railings and a tree-lined avenue. There's a black carriage going by with horses wearing plumed headdresses. It's an enclosed carriage with a lady inside wearing a powdered wig. I've entered a house that has a rather grand, almost spiral staircase and a marble hall. I'm walking up the stairs and I'm wearing very fancy, long, red pointed shoes, almost exaggerated like Mr Punch, with sort of white pom-pom things on the front. There's white hose on my legs, very *Liaison Dangereuse* kind of period. I've a doublet and ruffs round the neck and hips. There are two of us, a man and a woman, and they both keep merging into one, so I'm not sure which I am.'

Can you see yourself in the mirror?

'Oh, I'm the man. I'm wearing a powdered wig. I sleep in an intricate bedroom, it has a lot of fancy decor and a big four-poster bed with lots of gold motif on the bed head and masses of drapes. It's all very French, Marie Antoinette period; it doesn't have an English feel to it at all. There are a couple of sets of large green books and the writing is in French – it's definitely France.

'I own a perfumery. There are a lot of bottles, and clients in powdered wigs. I make these perfumes. It's a sort of shop-cum-salon: you can either buy a ready-made product or it can be designed to your own desires.'

We go back to when he was aged ten.

'I'm in a street. I'm a ragamuffin boy, very poor, wearing tattered clothes, just like *Les Miserables*. I live in a dirty house in a very poor area. There's a lady there who's cooking and pottering about in a pantry, quite countrified with no make-up and a roundish face. She's sort of a guardian, and I think it's an orphanage. I'm fairly happy. There's a man standing in the background in a powdered wig. He's quite smart and walks with a cane, very well-to-do, and he's talking to the woman. I think he visits regularly.'

We go forward to the age of fifteen.

'I'm working now, in a sort of iron works. I'm at an anvil banging and hammering; it's like a blacksmith's.'

We go to the time he leaves his poor circumstances.

'It's the well-to-do man – I feel as if he's snatched me. The lady isn't too well any more and he has come and taken me into his home and become my guardian. He's quite stern and I'm not especially happy to be with him, really, but there again I'm happy to get away from my old circumstances. It's a grand house and there's just the two of us.'

We go to age thirty.

'I'm very smart and sitting in a gambling house. There are elongated tables and fancy chairs; there's pool and cards and everything. I'm wearing a very smart outfit, but I'm actually very tense.'

We move on to when he was fifty.

'I'm quite plump. There's a large fire in the background and rather grand surroundings again, very ornate mirrors and candles, and there's a ball going on in the adjoining room. I'm in a powdered wig and just observing, I'm not joining in at all. I'm still running the perfumery. It's a very bright place and I'm happy there.

'My last memory is of being outside. I must be in my seventies. I'm looking under an ornate bridge at the reflections in the water. I feel as if the river is getting longer and longer. Now I feel like I'm something white and flying up into the sky and into the clouds.'

Tommy described the experience as very subtle, a little bit like dreaming but being awake. His apartment was very ornate and old-style French in decor and, of course, he was a very elegant man. He said that his desire for his own brand of perfume began years ago when he read a book about a perfumery and had been totally absorbed by it. This was particularly strange for him as he never read at all. He, like Elton John and Cynthia Lennon, adored Paris and used to take his holidays there every year.

It certainly seems that no experience is ever wasted, as in Lynsey's and Elton's progression in music. In my own case, I appear to be dedicated to the caring profession, and many times this has surfaced during the lives I have seen. After I had had my amazing cure for arthritis, I returned to the same regressionist and was shown a few more of my lives involving caring and nursing.

I saw yet another nun, this time in France and working in the slums with children and the sick. I even saw quite clearly that in past times I had worked as a healing nun using colour therapy. I saw my self placing sick people in a bed under a glass-type roof and for different illnesses we changed the colour of the glass. I even used various coloured glass bottles that I filled with water and placed in the sun and used as tonics. As I said earlier, the orthodox medical world is slowly adopting many of the practices of complementary medicine and colour therapy is amongst them. All-white hospital rooms are becoming rarer in favour of relaxing colours such as green, while strident colours such as red are avoided at all costs.

Another life that I described earlier and saw very vividly was that of a shaman in a Canadian Indian tribe. That particular life interlaced with my present time and had a great affect on me. In fact, as I mentioned before, I was amazed when I saw myself in a tepee with a fire in the middle of it – I never knew they had fires inside tepees – not to mention the fleas hopping in the fur bed rugs!

The other life that I was shown in regression therapy was that of a young girl in an Inca village. I was one of many young girls who were never put into normal life but kept in the confines of the temple since being a baby. From that time on I was taught to live a life of meditation and prayer. Then when still quite young I was taught to go off into a trance to bring messages for the temple leaders. I saw myself at the very end of this life, still a young girl, sitting at the front of a gathering of Inca men. They all had the same hair cut: straight to just below the ear and cut straight across. They were all swaying in rhythm and chanting, and as they swayed I felt myself going into a deep trance state. I then found myself trapped in darkness and had to be helped to the light. When in the light I was shown what happened. There had been an earth tremor bringing down large boulders on to the whole congregation and we had all died instantly. I had died in a trance state so was not even aware of what had happened. This life was shown to me when I had just begun working as a transfiguration medium and it seemed to have been brought forward to make this gift stronger. Strangely enough, about the same time as I was shown this life a friend showed me a picture of the remains of an ancient Inca village and straightaway I pointed to where the temple area was. He was quite amazed as on the following page was a map of the layout of this village and, sure enough, the religious area was exactly where I had said.

So in my case and many others, I see a definite pattern. It's as though each incarnation is only a practice at creating a totally fulfilling life.

Another celebrity who fitted into this theory was Uri Geller. He is famous for his spoon-bending abilities and for making broken clocks tick again. He also does a neat job of holding seeds in his hand for a few seconds until they actually begin to sprout. I had proof of his metal-bending prowess when he organised an event whereby he tuned into the whole of Britain at a specific time. It was run by one of the tabloid newspapers and I had read about it in the morning and thought nothing of it. I lived near Uri at that time, however, and that day we had gone out on our boat and had to pass his house to get to the pub where we had decided to moor up and have lunch. We finally found a good mooring spot and I went to turn off the engines only to discover that the key had bent double in the lock and the cork-floater key holder had shot across the room. So next time Uri does one of his many experiments, do avoid going anywhere near his home. He is a very wealthy man now as he got fed up with being called a fake and magician (which he is definitely not) and turned his hand to finding oil and minerals for companies just by being flown over huge areas and tuning into where he felt they should drill.

I went along to his house a few times and on my last visit he agreed to contribute to this project. I thought that he would be an easy subject as I assumed that to have built such power he must be an ardent meditator, so it came as a surprise to find he didn't even know how to meditate! Nevertheless he proved to be a wonderful subject. Here's what he saw.

'I'm a man wearing a long gold robe and slippers that curl up at the toes. I'm about twenty-five years old with black curly hair (which seemed to shake him). I'm walking down the stairs of a kind of dungeon with many arches. It's a kind of storage place with lots of compartments in the walls containing many large, thick scrolls of paper. I've headed to one particular compartment and taken out a small box. It has a chain with a cross on it. It feels and looks like a Christian cross, but on closer inspection I realise it meets in the middle unlike the Christian one.'

What he is referring to is actually one of the very earliest religious symbols, denoting the four aspects of man.

'The cross is hand-engraved. I don't know whether I'm to put the cross on or not.

'I see my days are spent partly in gardens with very narrow, long pools or ponds. It's very kind of Babylonian or Arabic in architectural style.

'For my work I see myself writing in a language I cannot identify. I can't identify the strange device I'm using for a pen either – it's something I've never seen before. I'm writing some kind of instructions, how to do something. I'm working in a building made up of huge blocks of stone, like a kind of monument. I'm watching other people drawing similar structures, architects of some kind.

'As a young boy I lived by the river. My mother wears a shawl over her head and my father is in armour with a brass chest plate. He has a beard and curly hair and very strong features. He's also wearing a helmet.'

Uri then recalled his school, and went on to reveal fascinating detail about the rest of this life.

'It's a big hall surrounded by lots of gardens and all the students, myself included, are wearing white robes with thick belts.

'At the age of thirty-five I find myself riding a horse across desert terrain. There are people following behind, leading donkeys carrying packages. We are off to board a boat, a biblical-style boat, and I feel we have sailed to Greece. It's an island where the locals greet us all. The men have beards and they are accompanied by women and children. They help unload the packages which are made up of bundles of papers from the boat. I think I have come to help build a structure like the one I worked on in my own country. It's squarish, huge, and has four supporting pillars. It's some sort of arena for observing things; I think it's to observe an operation.

'Now I'm seeing the building finished and in use. It's packed to capacity with adults; no children. They are all watching a gentleman sitting in the centre of the arena, crossed-legged in a kind of yogic position. He is of Indian origin with a towel spread out before his legs and is mixing various herbs. A lamb is brought before him and he puts a mixture into its eyes, a powdered mixture. It's a new kind of medicine for healing the lamb's eyes.

'I met the demonstrator through my friendship with another man from the same kind of country, India or Pakistan or Afghanistan maybe. I have, in the past, exchanged information with this man, and small, clear vases containing liquid that looked like medicines.

'At the age of forty-five I'm living in either a Greek or Turkish village. I'm some kind of leader, very looked up to. I'm instructing and helping the villagers in collecting water from a local waterfall to put into clay jars. The water is then taken to a square well. I feel it's for a kind of spiritual ceremony. The ceremony is held at night, but it is still light. There is a fire in the middle and I'm standing a short distance from it. There are small goblets containing the water being passed around to drink from. It's an open-air building filled with adults and their children. I appear to be like the local doctor because they are looking to me for help.'

We go towards the end of this life.

'I'm in a city in France, inside a building. There are many people around me who seem to be very interested in what I'm saying. They look very well-off people, many of them even look like royalty, wearing very expensive-looking robes. The building is a centre, my very own centre. I'm reading out loud to the people gathered round me.'

He appeared to have reached the end of this life, but could not see his death, so I asked him what he felt was his greatest achievement.

'The discovery of a new tablet. It appears to be made up of salt or similar compound. It has great healing powers and has freed many children from disease. A very fulfilled life.'

By this point Uri had gone into a very deep state of meditation, so I pushed forward to his next memory.

'I can see a blue-eyed Siamese-type cat. I'm wearing a black and white striped blouse – the stripes are actual stripes, not printed on to the material, they have gold or brass-type paint on them. I'm wearing something below that – it actually looks like a skirt – sandals on my feet and brownish rust-coloured hair. I'm male with very strong arms.

'I'm living in Italy, probably Rome, in a building made of huge stones; many of these are marble. I'm aged between thirty and forty. I'm holding a mixture of rubies, sapphires, emeralds and diamonds wrapped in a leather skin. I'm showing the stones to a very beautiful woman who is dressed in a thin, white, long, linen dress. Her hair is curly in front and smooth at the back. She finally chooses a large emerald, but it is not to be used as a jewellery item, but for her to concentrate on; it's employed for consulting the spiritual.

'I'm a warrior, belonging to a platoon of conquerors. We go to other countries seeking artefacts and precious stones for our collection.'

We go to the end of this life.

'I'm surrounded by fire; the whole place seems to be in flames. I'm helping other people to escape, but I'm trapped. The flames are getting worse . . .'

I manage to take him from the fire that he said he could feel, and lead him to the light. I ask him what he learned that time around.

'I gained knowledge of a kind of deeper prayer, a religion deeply set.'

When I got him into the light he saw his father who had at that time only recently passed over. As I've said before, this is a common occurrence for the recently bereaved. He was very surprised at how deeply he had gone into the experience, because as at first he felt he would be a bad subject. It was interesting to see that the mystical and spiritual appeared to run through his lives.

Also he is, like myself, an ardent collector of crystals. In fact, my own obsession with collecting crystals grew into my opening a specialist shop adjacent to my consultancy. Uri's magnificent home is spotted with huge stones, some of them very rare. He told me a story about his crystals that confirmed my findings of the great powers they hold. His house has a huge marble-tiled hallway with a minstrel gallery overlooking it. One day, when his son was only a tot, he heard a scream emanating from the hall and rushed out just in time to see his child fall from the gallery to what he thought would be his death on the marble floor below, but to his amazement he saw a sort of a starry beam glow from a six-foot tall crystal he had by the door. The beam seemed to hold the child and break his fall. He rushed over to find that the boy was not even bruised, just shocked. The crystal in question was the largest I have ever seen. He bought it at an auction at Christie's and it was ancient. I have witnessed many examples of the power of crystal and am not generally surprised by it, but this impressed even me.

I would have liked to have done another session with Uri as I felt that he probably had lives that link even more with the strange gift he has this time around. Mind you, the lives we saw were certainly unusual.

I know that this next example of a regression with a client may seem oddly placed in a chapter on talents, but in a way this particular regression applies equally well here. I had been treating a lady who had had a very bad time in her recent past. She had just been released from a clinic where she had been treated for heroin and alcohol addition. She was now clean and desperately trying to rebuild her shattered life. I mainly gave her healing and spiritual counselling, but one day she told me of an image she used to see when on heroin. She had really hit rock bottom and had taken to the streets as a prostitute to get money to feed her addiction. She told me that her bath had a large mirror by the side of it and about the time she had gone on to the streets, she began seeing herself in the mirror as a horrible old hag. I decided to regress her to see if my feelings on why this might have happened were right.

She came up in a life when the rich drove around the city in horse-drawn coaches. She had had a very rough upbringing and had finally become a woman of the night. She saw herself frequenting a part of London that had huge arches and she saw men picking her up in their carriages, or from local inns. She eventually ended her life in poverty and saw herself as the same old hag who had been overshadowing her in the present life.

After the session she told me of her amazement that the arches she had used to parade her wares all those years ago were the same arches that she had taken to recently. When she had fallen on hard times and was desperate for money, she had gone into a past memory trap and had more or less become that girl she was so very long ago, only this time trading her wares in taxis.

So, as we saw there, it's not always talents that are brought forward from one life to another. Often something that has made an impression on this life is brought to the fore to help the person understand themselves.

One such example was Susan Devoy from New Zealand, the world champion squash player, a title she held for six consecutive years. This is what she saw during regression.

'I'm in a huge dining room with old furniture, tables and tall slatted windows with bars. I can't see out of the windows because they are too high up. It's England in the 1800s. I sleep in a dormitory with lots of bunk beds. I'm about ten years old and wearing a nightshirt; my feet are bare. I'm in a sort of boarding school, and I feel as though I've been here since time began. I hate it. It's an orphanage.

'I was born in a huge house. Mother cleans in the kitchen. I sleep in a big box.

'After leaving the orphanage, I go to work as a

general dogsbody in a hotel. When I'm eighteen I'm serving drinks behind the bar, but I get into a big row with the manager and end up fighting. I'm consequently thrown out on to the streets to live rough and sleep rough. I can't get work or food! I get weaker and weaker and can't function.'

She dies at this point of starvation, so I take her to the light and push her forward to see what I hope will be a better life.

'I'm sitting beneath a huge Christmas tree. It's lavishly trimmed with lights, toys and other gifts. There are lots of jolly people, family and friends.

'I'm a boy aged about five. It's America, in the countryside near Boston. My mother is a housewife and very lovely. My father is a financier in the city; I feel it's in New York. I'm an only child and have lots of toys and everything. I go to school in a small barn-like building. I like it. I love football and want to play a lot.

'When I leave school I go to work in a law office. I do well in my career and move forward quickly. By the time I'm twenty-two I die suddenly. I'm at a meeting sitting around a large boardroom table. In the middle of the meeting I collapse and die. I don't know what from, I wasn't ill at all before this.'

We never did find the cause of this death, as it was so sudden that there were no clues in the soul memory, but it looked like a heart attack. She did go straight to the right place, to the light, so we pressed on to Susan's next and last regression memory.

'I'm wearing riding clothes and standing at a stable

door. I'm a girl about fourteen years old, and my clothes are side-saddle style. I live in a huge house – we're a titled family. My mother is a very frilly person in hooped skirts and corseted-style dress. I don't like her much; I think she's a wimp. Father wears knickerbocker-style leggings and waistcoat; he is quite young and dashing. I adore him, but yet I'm quite afraid of him. His grandfather was a baron. No one works other than running our huge estate.

'Most of my young life is spent partying and playing. I'm very much a tomboy and hate being lady-like, but I am kept very strictly. I'm a bit of a rebel and long to break away.

'Out riding one day I meet a man, also on horseback. I fall in love with him but he's a gambler and no good. My parents ban me from seeing him because he's most unsuitable. I run away at the dead of night on the back of his horse. We live in squalid conditions. He's very bad to me. He beats me and hardly ever comes home at nights. I have two children by him and live in a meagre cottage toiling, fetching wood and so on. I'm desperately unhappy.

'Eventually my father dies and I'm sent for to attend the funeral. By this time my mother has gone weird and is not in control of herself. I move back to live and look after her and look after the children and run the estate.

'I appreciate this life now, but have become very bossy and rigid as estate manager. I sit in a huge office most of the day.

'My children have children and make me a grandmother. I live to a very old age and die surrounded by loving family in a huge four-poster bed.'

Susan told me later that in this life she is a compulsive eater and says one of her ambitions in life is to be able to eat till she bursts! All her friends know her for her eating and make jokes about it. At buffets she just can't leave the food table. This must be a hangover from her dying of starvation. It is a frequent occurrence that those who have suffered this form of death in a past life have excessive eating habits in this. Susan also commented after the three sessions that she never seemed to have grown up or felt properly matured in any of her lives, and said she felt she hadn't in this life either.

Amongst other celebrities who saw past talents was an actor called Ken Parry. Although his name is perhaps not familiar, his face almost certainly would be, as he has had parts in many films and television shows, including the Taylor and Burton film *The Taming of The Shrew*, the part of Fat Eric in *The Sweeney*, as well as many more roles. I wanted to regress Ken for several reasons. Firstly, he is very well-known to most people in show business and is a great source of amusement to all who have had the pleasure of working with him. But my main reason for wanting to have this session was because he is well known as a psychic and keeps all his fellow thespians amused by calling up his guide, chatting with him openly and giving spirit messages to all and sundry. Michael Cashman, the actor who is best known for his role of Colin in the TV soap *EastEnders*, told me of a time on tour with him when he actually had an argument with his guide, a Native American, and loudly declared to the air, 'Don't you flash your tail feathers at me! Just you come back here now!' I was therefore not surprised when he turned out to be quite an unusual sitter who was able to give tremendous detail in his regression, such as names and places. Ken whisked briskly through four lives at his home in London and I'll just print them as they occurred.

'I'm looking at a very big portal and a very big door with steps leading to it. They are stone steps with

no banister. It's the front of the house. There's a huge knocker. I reach out to knock on the door and my arm is the very delicate arm of a young girl. I'm wearing a kind of cape in grey. I have very shiny patent leather shoes with a gold buckle and a long dress. I think it's the early 1800s. I'm eighteen and have auburn hair and am very pale and wan.

'I'm let into the house by a man wearing livery who takes me up the staircase. The staircase is brown and is decorated with pictures of people. I'm taken to a bedroom and there's this lovely-looking young man waiting for me; he's stripped to the waist. I take off my cloak and he kisses me. He's my boyfriend.

'I live in a little cottage not far from him in the country. My father has grey hair and smokes a long clay pipe; he's old and retired. I look after him. He used to be a doctor and the house has many medical books on the shelves.'

We go forward to the age of thirty-five.

'I'm out in the fields watering flowers. I'm a spinster because my boyfriend was killed in the war, serving with the Duke of Wellington's regiment. I work as a teacher: I teach children literature at St Mark's Infants School. It's 1864. I'm a regular churchgoer and lead a pretty uneventful life.'

We go to the end of this life.

'I'm a very old maid. I'm sitting in a chair talking to a lady friend. There's a sharp pain in my chest and I'm gone.'

I was amazed at the way he reeled off dates and names;

this kind of detail is quite unusual. There was no need for a rescue as the soul had died peacefully, so we moved straight into the next vision. In any session, the subject goes deeper and deeper into their soul memory as the regression progresses, so I was wondering what detail this man would come up with next!

'It sounds silly but I'm standing at the bottom of a staircase and I'm a very young and glamorous young man and I know it's silly and doesn't connect but I'm singing to Jeanette Macdonald who's in a crinoline at the top of the stairs. I'm singing waltz songs with her and laughing. I'm very happy. I can't make the vision go away. I've got the most lovely blonde hair and I can see my skin is lovely. I'm wearing a sort of page boy outfit, but I'm not a page. I'm seventeen or eighteen. I'm on the stage and I can now see that the woman is not Jeanette Macdonald but she's very like her. I think this is about 1900. I've got a carriage and horses and I'm very successful and I live in Eton Square.'

We go out to see the front of the theatre he is playing at.

'It's The Gaiety. The front boards say "George Edwards presents Flora Dora starring Harry Elvin", that's me.'

I ask if he has heard of him.

'No, I haven't but that's my billing, I can see.'

We go back to the age of ten.

'I'm by the sea with my mother and father who are obviously professional artists. They are a magic act called "The Two Elvins". I can see a little music stand at the side of the stage with their names on it. At the age of five I was put on to the stage with five other children wearing sailor costumes. It's not in London, it's Bury St Edmunds.'

We move on to middle age in this life.

'I go to America by boat. I stay in Boston and decide to settle down there and teach singing – I've a very good voice and became very famous. I marry an American girl and have three children, Claude, Bridget and Carol.'

We go to the end of this life.

'I'm still in Boston and I'm in my seventies. I have a stoop and am a very distinguished person with people all around me paying their respects. There's an obituary in the paper, the *Boston Echo*, I can see it, it says "Harry Elvin dies at seventy-two". It's dated 1929.'

I am by now, as you can imagine, quite flabbergasted as Ken has gone straight to the light each time. So we press on.

'I'm being plunged and plunged and plunged right down to the bottom of the sea. I'm lost. I'm really lost. Everything's spinning around.'

Try to focus on something like your clothes.

'Yes, I can see a pair of check trousers, it's a check suit. Everything keeps ebbing and flowing and changing.'

You have obviously died at sea.

'Yes, I definitely drowned but I can't seem to get out of the water.'

We concentrate on seeing the situation clearly.

'I can see it now. I was buried at sea wrapped in a hammock.'

I take the whole thing into the light and clear his confusion.

'Yes, yes, I can see him clearly now and he's bright and cheerful.'

This experience is very common in my work when lives that have not been cleared and need help come forward right at the end of the session. I know that he had died and not gone to the light, hence his feeling of swirling about in the sea, as he was still with his body. The reason for that was probably that he met with a sudden death whilst in shock. His last life went back to being very precise again and in no need of rescue. Here it is.

'I can smell the strong aroma of garlic. I know I'm in France. I hate to say it but I'm wearing a frock again: it's very elegant with diamanté on it and I'm wearing a powdered wig. There are lovely white horses outside. I'm in my twenties and we've got servants. It's absolutely gorgeous. There's a lot of land and a big drive before you get to the house. I'm speaking in French! I'm married but don't have any children yet.'

We go back ten years.

'I'm in Rouen in some kind of general store and I'm behind the counter watching my father serve people – it's an everything kind of store. I'm fourteen and live in the city of Leonne. By the time I'm fifteen I'm being instructed in science, it's a mixed class. I can see the Bunsen burners and things like that. I live at 52 Roux Avrone; it's a white building and there's a concièrge. I share an apartment with a girl called Elaine. I met my husband there; he's studying to be a doctor and I was studying medicine, too. My parents wanted me to have a good education, we were middle class.

'The wedding was really wonderful with carriages and footmen, then afterwards we went to live in Provence. He became a famous surgeon called Henri Laseur. He specialised in abdominal surgery. We later move to the sea, Toulouse, and we have four children. I spend my days walking by the sea and doing needlework and tapestries. I have lots of lady friends and give tea parties. My husband is a very busy man so I don't see much of him. I remain in Toulouse till I die. My husband was given an honour, he achieved distinction for his services, a sort of French knighthood. Our home is in a fishing village. We lost one child, André, from typhoid. My husband died before me in a place called Riex. I was still very sound. My husband was a lot older than me. I died of a cough which led to bronchial pneumonia.'

I don't suppose I need to say that he didn't need me to take him to the light as he was quite capable of finding his own way! I was left breathless after these sessions, astounded by his remarkable memory, far memory that is. I wondered if it was because of his psychic abilities that he saw things so clearly. I used to go regularly to give healing to the psychic Doris Stokes when she was alive; I just wish I had regressed her!

I had already had an experience of regression with another psychic years earlier. I used to work with a very good trance medium who is an excellent clairvoyant and hypnotist. We had toured together and done a lot of healing demonstrations in Florida. I had met him in his capacity as a trance medium and had become great friends with him and his family, even sharing holidays with them. His wife had asked me if I would do some regression sessions with him to try to clear what she felt was a blockage that was severely affecting his home life.

The first session was astonishing as the moment I brought in the power he slumped forward into a trance state and I was amazed when, a moment later, he sat up and began singing a Native American tribal song. He spoke in the language of the Native American, in fact he quite literally became that man. He finally ceased his singing and slumped forward once more, but then sat back up and was taken over by his guide who informed me that my sitter had been a chief in the Cree Indian tribe and that I had been his blood brother, the shaman. So here I was in the midst of my normal working day and once more I was being confronted with one of my own past lives that I knew so well. It was wonderful to find out where I had known my sitter from before, as in this life we have the same sense of humour and are even the same star sign, our birthdays being within a couple of days of each other, and we are great friends – I now realise, forever.

Another person who used to come to me for healing was Fenella Fielding, the actress with the wonderful gravelly voice so famous for her many roles including the vamp in *Carry On Screaming*. The very first time she came to see me turned out to be hilarious. She came to me for healing because she felt she had something seriously wrong with her feet. I laid my hands on her and kept getting the impression of shoes, so I asked her if she had some new shoes. Realisation suddenly dawned on her face. She had just taken over the lead in a play and they had given her the last person's shoes and outfits! She had to laugh, as she felt such a fool for not realising that for herself. However, it did make for a good relationship between healer and patient as she knew from that moment on that I was genuine. I did a few regressions with her and she has given me permission to relay them to you. She saw four lives and here they are.

'I see a door with raised pattern in kind of stone material on dark, heavy-looking wood with a large brass handle. I'm in a courtyard with pale-coloured, bleached out walls with blue and pink decorations. It's paved with large coloured stones and there are square archways and narrow pillars. There is bright sunlight and donkeys pottering about. It seems to be an entrance courtyard leading to various houses. There are a few people about wearing loose clothing and loose trousers, warm weather clothes. They all have Mexican-type skins and dark hair mostly wearing Mexican-shaped hats. There are narrow cobbled streets – it's a very simple place.

'I'm wearing sandals with thick leather soles. I'm a man with blousey trousers in creamy chrome colour and a loose shirt tucked in, open at the front. I'm also wearing a hat – I think we have to because of the heat.

'My house is small and dark to keep the sun out. There's a plump lady there at a large wooden table sitting on a bench seat with a scarf over her head in a kind of Indian style. There are two boys wearing knee-length trousers, thin and loose, with small brimmed hats. I feel we are in Peru.

'I'm a shoemaker. I work with a metal foot to build them on; I shape the leather over it. They are simple shoes, very soft, and I sell them in the market place. It's a colourful place with walls made of tiny bricks, very narrow with decoration up at the top. The ground is very dry and there are kids, goats, for sale and very bright coloured fruit, melons and pumpkins. Masses of colour. The shoes are similar to moccasins, a very gathered sort of style. I go to a special place to buy the skins where they are hung over a wall, some stained with dye and some not.

'I go to a high mountain where I can just see the villages through the heat mists. There are old women, dressed in black from head to toe, nipping about – they don't look strong enough to be rushing about, but they are.

'I die young, but the life gave me a feeling of continuity and appreciation of the elements. I die in a bed surrounded by my family from babies to old folk.'

I did not have to help in any way with this end as the whole situation was surrounded by the light of the family's love. Clearly this was another case where a talent had moved through to this life, as Fenella said later,

'It is extraordinary, really. I sat for hours one day riveted in Rodney Fried's ballet shoe shop and watched him work away making these ballet shoes and adored seeing the love that was going into his skill. But long before that I went to an exhibition in some big place in Piccadilly where they had eleventh-century clothing and they had some actual shoes from then, and I found them very touching because, except for a few things we have now, they were made in exactly the same way I had made them in the Peruvian life. In fact I get absolutely magnetised by beautifully made shoes. I found it strange that I knew it was Peru as I have never been there, and I felt it was most significant that I knew it was there and not somewhere like Spain. I did used to love things from the Mexicana shop, and at one time practically everything I had was from there.'

It is quite common for my subjects to be amazed that they know the name of the place they are seeing. It comes to them in a kind of clairvoyant way; the name of the place just pops into their minds. Actually it is their own soul memory telling them where. The fact that her tastes were at one time drawn to Mexico is again very common as the more regressions people have, the more they realise that many of their tastes originate from past lives. The next life Fenella saw was just one to clear away, so we can leave it here to show the continuity of the session rather than use it to illustrate the theme.

'I'm walking up a wooden staircase that leads to a lovely attic room where I like to go and sit. It's a loft where I can be absolutely quiet and peaceful, and it feels very secret. There is a lovely view of gardens. I'm wearing a longish dress but it's short really for the time. I'm a teenager. It's a Victorian-style dress. I'm very happy and have chestnut hair and am able to kick off my shoes here. I like that.

'My parents are some kind of gentry. Dad's wearing mid-brown Holland material britches and narrow trousers; he's very nice. We live in a big house in the country – I think it's England. It's a flat-fronted house, rather wide with columns, quite an unusual house, very simple but very big. My parents are well off but not exceptionally rich. Dad doesn't seem to work – well not with his hands anyway – but he has many hobbies.

'At the age of twenty, I'm married and still live in the country in the same house with my parents. My husband is a teacher at the local school, teaching reading as well as other things. I cook a lot; I'm a very young wife. I also help my husband at the school, teaching. It's a small school, not what you would call a village school, though, just a small school in the country. We have fifteen pupils in our class.

'At the age of forty I feel life is very quiet. I'm
seeing cows and fields and my circumstances have
changed. My husband died ages ago: he got a
fishing hook caught in his leg and the injury didn't
get better. I'm very lonely. I live in a much smaller
house with pink roses round the door; it's a cottage.
Everything looks very brown as if things have died.
I became quite poor as a result of widowhood. I
spend my time sewing, but mostly I'm alone.
'I'm in a wheelchair in the garden – it's a dark
garden . . .'

At this point I guided her to the light.

'I don't feel anything happened in this life – it was
a slight waste. The nicest part was my childhood
and my early marriage.'

On feeling her sadness, I naturally took her to another
memory to redress the balance of this one.

'I'm looking at a large eye. I'm very close to a quiet
old man with grey curly hair and something
swathed round his head – he's a shepherd. I'm a
woman wearing saffron-coloured robes in a crinkly
material. I'm in Egypt. It's bright sunlight and
desert, I don't see it as desert, though. The houses
have painted roofs and columns, not very closed in
at all. I'm living in a very spacious place
surrounded by walls that are not like walls and are
made of cones or something. It's so big I can't even
see it all. My room has a window but no glass. It
seems to be stone and mosaic, and it has wall
hangings, but it's not elaborate, just comfortable.
I'm a girl of sixteen and I'm with a man of about
forty. He's wearing loose draped clothes, he's got

large eyes and large eyelids and straight, dark, medium-length hair cut just below his ears and scraped back from the forehead. My hair is dark and crinkly and long. I know I have no mother, in fact I feel I'm an orphan. The man I'm with is quite important. I feel he keeps the accounts and everything in order and looks after his business in general. He has to be referred to all the time, without being pompous, he's just in a very responsible position. My mother died soon after I was born and I can hardly remember my father. I feel I'm looked after by this man.

'At the age of twenty I'm still at the same place. I've become part of the household and the man has taught me to deal with lots of things in the household. I work with figures like him. There are lots of staff but they are below me in position. I'm able to command them because of who I am. I don't feel I'm any kind of princess but it's just being with this man that makes me important.

'I'm forty years old and I now realise I'm married to this man.'

We go back to the age of six to find out more of her history.

'I'm in a small place which makes me think of a piece of honeycomb, like those candles that are made like honeycomb. I'm being taken from this place to somewhere to be looked at, it's as if I've been sold. When my mother died and father got killed I feel that I was sold. I don't feel sad about it; it seems to be a very normal thing to be done. I'm in a room with a lot of other children of my age. I don't know who the other children are.

'At the age of ten I'm entrusted with messages to take outside; I've been picked out for this.'

When and where did you meet the man you later married?

> 'I'm fourteen and I'm sitting on my bed thinking
> about things and someone comes to my room and
> takes me along to see him. I know I'm being
> looked at, sort of like an interview. I feel very
> respectful of the situation, not nervous.'

Go to the wedding and tell me about it.

> 'There are very low ceilings with lots of lattice work
> and lots of old incense-type things. I'm wearing a
> sort of cap that covers my head but not all of my
> hair – it's heavily embroidered and beaded. The
> dress is like a pretty shift, white in colour, but it's
> what I've got on my head that's important. He is
> wearing a light colour with a deep-coloured stripe
> down the side, it's loose to below the knee.
>   'At the age of fifty he's been dead a long time
> and I have two daughters to take care of; they are
> of marriageable age. I'm very old when I die.'

She goes straight to the light.

> 'I feel almost nothing and I was not alone. I feel
> very content because I have done everything I
> could have possibly done and have enjoyed my life.
> I feel I had a very fulfilling life for what was
> accepted then for a woman and on top of that I
> was given the privilege of having some learning.'

I was about to wind up this sitting when she rolled
straight into another life, so I went with the stream.

> 'What I can see now is very familiar, but I can't
> think what it's called. Lots of trumpets all tied

together on a wall – heraldic, that's the word. It's not a picture, it's real!'

Have you seen the heraldic trumpets often?

'It's funny because I didn't think I did, but now I think I do. They seem very familiar; I feel I see them when in half-sleep state, though. I'm seeing a sunset, but it's not dark. I'm seeing men in armour with steel helmets that go up to points. The men are on horseback, mostly greys and piebald. The sun is reflecting off their armour and also off the sea. It's not a war but they are in armour and they are on a cliff top. I'm about fifty yards away from them. I'm standing in the grass wearing something long. I'm female; I've got long fair hair in braids, like long, twisted bunches. I'm married to one of the riders. It's a medieval scene.

'I live in the country by the sea. I think it's England because I feel I'm definitely not in France. I live in a castle. My bedroom has a large bed in it and one window. The room is very light and I'm definitely not poor. I'm about twenty.

I ask her to describe her wedding, as these can tell us a lot about social standing and the time when the life took place.

'I'm in a small but tall church. I'm wearing something very pale and a circlet hat. He is wearing deep red, dark leggings. My dress is very simple. After my marriage I spend my days at the castle doing tapestries for wall hangings; they are stretched across a tall frame on a stand. It's not an active life. My husband is away most of the time and he never takes me with him. When he is next home there is to be a banquet with many people.

We are not giving it, someone else is. There is lots of food served on long tables. I'm very contented. I'm sitting near my husband but not next to him.

'By the time I'm thirty-five he's been killed in battle. I pace about a lot. There are lots of widows. Lots of company but it's not nice. By the time I reach forty-five I'm much more covered up than I used to be. I don't think I work, I don't do tapestry any more either. I go out a lot. I see myself as rather large and swathed in outdoor clothing. I do some sort of good works: I sit by sick beds and help nurse people. I get great satisfaction from it. I know a lot about herbs and things. It's something I never wanted to do but was led into it by a holy person, but I found I was rather good at it. I visit all sorts of people but all of my own class.'

Let's go to the end of your life.

'I'm not yet fifty-five, and I'm walking along a country lane and just become faint and fall over.'

She goes to the light.

'It was not horrid or violent. I still can feel the pleasure of being married to someone nice, also the good thing again of gaining knowledge and being able to use it and see the results.'

Fenella told me later that she fears being alone. She felt the second life had given her that fear. She also feels she has a healing power, something again which had transferred from a former life, and she has sought to learn more about this field. She often finds she knows what is wrong with people. She also finds herself very drawn to Egypt and says she has seen that same man that she married in that life in a kind of meditation. He was, she felt, a most wonderful man who, as she put it, 'took her out of the chorus line'.

CHAPTER SIX

❖

Variety is the
Spice of Lives

I have grown accustomed to the shock many people experience when they find they were a different sex or colour in the past – some try to dispute the evidence of their own meditative experience – so I found it very refreshing when I was invited to a luncheon and was seated next to the actress Joanna Lumley. When we began talking about regression, she declared with complete conviction that she felt sure she had been a man in her past life.

Someone else who didn't seem surprised to have been a male in a past life was Sharron Davis the Olympic swimming champion and now Gladiator Amazon. I must admit I wasn't either. After watching her on *Gladiators* she certainly still has the beating of most men! At the session in her home, it was quite hard to get her into a deep state of meditation, and although I did eventually get her away, she found it difficult to hold the visions, so we only covered one life. I know she had been training earlier and I don't think a person who's body is still awash with adrenaline makes the perfect subject. Anyway I'll relay it now as it came.

'I'm seeing a place that looks like the West Country in England with fields and trees. My feet are medium size and have very strappy leather sandals on them. They look like a man's feet! I'm walking towards a place that looks like an old castle, all stone with lots of trees and grass right up to it. It's quite large and there's a drawbridge. I'm walking across it and I can see water below the bridge. I'm going through a rounded entrance. It's very busy indeed inside, there are horses everywhere and a market going on. There's straw on the floor and the people seem to be wearing clothes made out of sacking. There are lots of chickens for sale. It's just an ordinary market with lots of carts and activity. I think it's medieval. It's surrounded by a stone wall and the wall leads to more walls and then a sort of turret. I can see a sword: it's a really big, strong, heavy, iron sword and I think it belongs to me, although it's resting up against the wall. I think I'm wearing red heraldry-type clothes, a sort of tunic. There's a really large, tall, white horse wearing blinkers and one of those sort of pelmet things that they put over horse's backs. It all seems very vague and I'm having to try very hard.

'I keep seeing a little hill and there's only me there. I'm riding the horse and I seem to be looking at the whole thing from quite high up. I can't seem to see anything after this hill. I feel as if I'm sitting on this horse and it's just walking up the hill. When I look down to the ground, though, I can see a silver-coloured helmet with a nose shield and on top a flag that is white with a gold cross on it.'

Sharron could not see anything beyond this, but I knew it was her death and the fact that she appeared to be in armour could probably mean she died in battle. This makes her position as a Gladiator more interesting as it seems to be something she knows from her far memory. I think perhaps it might daunt some of her competitors in the show if they realised that she had been trained to kill in a past life. I wonder if that memory being brought forward helped in these contests? I knew she was not trapped in darkness so did not need to press her further.

One of the most adamant denials of ever being a man came from the actress Vivienne Ventura – she just could not accept the possibility. I had gone to her house in London, and only managed to do the regressions with great difficulty, as she is such a busy person – in fact, I had to go back twice. The first time I visited the house I was let in by a maid and was shown into the lounge – an amazing room that made me feel as though I was in a nightclub! After sitting there politely for about an hour, by which time I was beginning to feel that I ought to scream of my presence, one of Vivienne's daughters came in and looked surprised to see me. When I told her what I was waiting for she went off saying she would alert her mother. It was yet another hour later when Vivienne herself walked into the room and exclaimed in astonishment that no one had told her I was there! By that time I was in no mood for doing any work, as not only was I very close to my next appointment, my parking ticket was about to expire, so we arranged another time. I must say that she was devastated at the mistake, and we were both delighted that when we finally did the session it went very well.

> 'I'm seeing a huge wooden door, a very antique one.
> It's Spanish in style with lots of engravings on it
> with an enormous round handle right in the centre.
> You don't open the door by the handle, though, it
> has this huge keyhole in it. Inside there's a patio
> with beautiful trees growing and fountains. All the
> rooms give out on to this patio. I've not seen this
> particular place before but I have seen many like it.
> The house almost seems inside out, as the garden is
> in the centre surrounded by the house. It seems to be
> the nineteenth century but the house is much older,
> probably two hundred years more.

'The hand I can see is that of a male and he's wearing espadrilles and white cotton trousers; he's in his mid thirties. He's going to a terrace on the upper floor; I think he lives there.'

Up to this point, Vivienne doesn't seem to think she is this man, but when I asked her why he is going up the stairs, she begins to refer to him as 'I', before reverting back to 'he'.

'I'm going there for peace, tranquillity, freshness and coolness. It's his house but he doesn't live there all the time, it's just one of his houses. He breeds horses and has olive groves. I think it could be in South America.

'As a child he lived on a farm with his very wealthy parents and was educated by private tutors. He has grown into a very handsome man. He never married and spends most of his relaxation time riding horses alone or with friends.

'By the time he is fifty-five he has moved to the tropics and still rides horses and listens for hours to the opera. He is extremely rich and now doesn't do any work at all. He appears to be in Columbia in South America. He's in a beautiful old house that overlooks the sea, situated in an old town. My last memory of him is looking out to sea and then he's gone.'

He went straight to the light and we went straight on with the next memory.

'There's heat and dust and music. I feel it's somewhere in the Middle East. I'm wearing lots of rings: they're not precious stones, well, they could be but they're not sort of big diamonds or emeralds, they're more ornamental. I'm female and am wearing a fedora and am in a big tent.'

I noted there was an immediate acceptance of this person, since she is female.

'I'm about twenty years old. There are lots of other women with me in the tent. The tent is covered in Persian rugs. It's very hot. The rest of the women are family, I think.

'As a child I was brought up with my parents. They were very mysterious people. My mother hardly ever spoke and had very few teeth. My father always wore a very ornamental kaftan and spent a lot of his time sitting around with other men and never seemed to have any time for my mother. I can still smell his clothes; they smelt very badly of goats and camels.

'The tent I am in now smells of rosewood, a very strong smell of roses. We burn incense and the heat increases the smell. I sit around most of the day and gossip with the other women. I'm very happy. I am married but my husband is away a lot. He's a trader in spices and perfumes and travels for his work and I am never taken with him.

'At the age of thirty we are travelling across the desert. I have children and life seems to be very normal to me. We have travelled many miles to a camp by the sea – it looks like Morocco or somewhere. My husband is trading there and has taken us all with him this time. He has stopped travelling and intends to trade in this one place.

'By the time I am fifty we are still in the same area. I'm very tired now, though. My husband never travels any more; he has people to travel his wares for him. He is very rich by now. I die soon after this. I am in the tent surrounded by family and people.'

Again, the soul went straight to the light, a most uncomplicated lady. Vivienne later said how interesting the whole thing was as her ancestors were Jewish nomads from the Middle East; her family were Moors. She still feels she does the same thing in this life, as she travels all the time, only this time by first class jet plane. She is also very sensitive to smells, as her regression brought forward. She still uses incense in her home and is very interested in Arab countries and culture, and says she always feels very much at home there.

The horse riding she feels she has brought to this life, as she still loves to ride; it gives her an incredible feeling. She never rides with boots and the rest of the gear as she cannot stand the restriction, but loves to ride on the Spanish beaches. In fact, she is addicted to the hot climate of Spain and South America, and loves Spanish music.

She found it hard to believe that she had ever been a man, and protested afterwards that she felt she was far too feminine to have ever been one. When I pointed out how clearly she saw him, she finally had to accept that the man was herself, but she pointed out that he never married and was exceedingly sensitive, so she could only conclude that he must have been gay! I feel that if she comes back as a man next time, that could well be the case.

Variety in gender is one interesting element of regression; variety in colour is another, as witnessed not only by Vivienne's swarthy South American looks, but by other celebrities who have been regressed. Nona Hendryx of the American recording artists 'LaBelle' (formerly Patti LaBelle and the Bluebells) was highly amused when she came up in a life as a white woman, as a few years earlier we had swapped 'roles' for a party at Elton John's house: Nona made up to look white, and me to look black! We were in Los Angeles for the celebrations and launch of Rocket Records over there, and we went to the Max Factor film make-up studio in Hollywood and got all the correct make-up including a wonderful Afro wig for me and long flowing blonde tresses for Nona. Mind you, in another of her lives we saw she was an exotic Arabian dancer, which could explain her taste for some of her outlandish stage costumes in the present. We went through four lives, in two of which she was white.

'I'm staring at a door I've never seen before. It has a latch and has lace behind the glass window in it. I reach out my hand and it's a female hand with soft leather gloves. I'm wearing a fancy eighteenth-century style dress: it's red with purple and black lace, large puffy sleeves and a full skirt. I'm English, aged about twenty-nine. I'm not black I'm white! (We stifle laughter!) I've got blonde hair under my hat. I'm very frightened about going through this door; I feel if I do I'll fall down. I just can't bring myself to open it.'

We leave the door for a while and look at her earlier in this life.

'I'm about twenty now. I can see the English countryside. My house is an ordinary cottage made of brick. My family is inside: father and mother, also my brother and sister. My father works in a bank and my mother is a housewife. I have lots of friends.
'I've gone to twenty-five now and I'm somewhere in London, in a house feeling good. I ride a lot. I'm married now and my husband is a businessman, a lawyer, and we have two children. It's a good and happy life. I can't really tell whether it's a flat or a house we live in. The house has a black front door, it's quite tall and in a nice, quiet street.'

We return to the door she was afraid of.

'I've gone inside – it's a party. There's a man there I

have to see, but he's not my husband. Something horrible is going on but I have to go in. I'm back home now and in my bedroom crying over a letter addressed to me, "Dear Marian . . .". It says it was all a mistake, the affair we had. I can remember everything now. That's why I was afraid of going into the room and facing him: the party had been his wedding reception.

'After the wedding I've run away to commit suicide.'

She then goes into extreme darkness and after we clear her of that she sees herself clearly again.

'I can see myself in a bright light and I'm with my boyfriend again. He's a soldier, and we're together again.'

I was pleased to be able to clear that life, as the suicide had trapped her in the dark memory. Her next life threw her back to being darker skinned.

'I can see the entrance to a cave and there are people inside. From the inside, I can look out over trees, tropical trees, it's jungle, it's the rainforest! I'm a girl with brown skin, not black but light brown. I don't wear much – only skins. My hair is soft, long, lush, straight and black. I'm barefoot. The people inside are dressed like me, and they are cooking and sitting around. I'm nineteen. My parents were killed by this tribe and I was taken by them. I have a dark memory of being dragged away screaming. I do nothing all day. We eat a lot of berries. I am forced to sleep with the man who is in charge; I don't like him but I have no choice.

'Years later I'm in the same jungle but in a

different home. I still don't like to be with these people because I come from a more sensitive, intelligent tribe.

'By the end of my life I have settled down more, I've had to. I now have three children and I'm happy with them. I know that I'm dying, but it's of natural causes.'

Life three came through almost instantly so I just relaxed and went with the flow.

'I'm floating above a wonderful, elegant room; it seems to be French. I'm wearing a robe. It all has to do with religion. It's a red robe with gold on it and I'm wearing a large, plain, gold cross. I'm in my forties with grey hair and a beard. I'm very happy. I sleep in a big room where there are lots of drapes, curtains, a mirror and my bed is huge, a huge wooden bed. The accommodation is part of a rich estate, and there's a small chapel which is very beautiful situated within the main house. The house is huge with big doors and arches. It's a summer's day. There are lots of people outside as an elaborate carriage arrives, which is met by the servants who are dressed very plainly. The people who get out of the coach are dressed in frilly, fussy clothes of velvet and satins. The men are wearing wigs. They are going into the house – they live there. I take their services in the little chapel, just for the family and servants.'

We go back to the age of ten.

'I can see a cottage in the grounds of another house. My father is a very religious man but he is not in the church, he wears peasant clothing. His wife is not my mother, she died in childbirth and I can't remember her. He works as a labourer on the estate of this other house. As a teenager I studied at the chapel with the priest because I wanted to enter the priesthood.

'After I'm ordained I go to sea. I can see myself on board a ship full of soldiers and we are going to war. I'm their chaplain, and we are going to Spain to fight. We are captured and imprisoned there. I share a cell with the soldiers, but we are helped to escape by a priest, and we had to walk miles to a Spanish monastery to hide. We're there a long time and we are happy with the monks and I begin writing about religious practices.

'There's a famine in France and I eventually go back to Paris to help. I'm in an elaborate church tending the sick. I'm not a very important priest but I gain a promotion. I'm then sent as a priest to the chapel where I was brought up. It's a good and comfortable life.

'At the end of the life I am back in Paris being bathed. I've come back here to take a better position in the church. I'm wearing a white and gold robe, it's sort of brocade, and I'm wearing two hats: a skull cap and a sort of flat hat. My last job was in administration but I am being prepared to die now.'

I felt that when she first came in on this one and was floating above a room, that she was already dead, but I brought her into the life so we could investigate further. Then again she zoomed off into yet another life. I feel this next one had a great bearing upon this present life. As you will know if you have ever seen LaBelle perform, they are very exotic and sensual – so let me show you where she originally got her training.

'I'm in an alleyway outside a door with a light over the top. I go through the door and I'm backstage in a beautiful theatre. It's empty except for a few people wandering about near the stage. They are all Middle Eastern people, brown-skinned. The theatre is very elaborate with designs of elephants and lots of bright colours in red-gold and pink. It has a very big, rounded ceiling also brightly painted.

'I'm going on to the stage now. I'm wearing lots of flimsy veils and another veil over my face. I'm a dancer – I dance the seven veils! I'm very young, I'm only about sixteen at the most.'

We go back to the age of seven.

'I'm in the desert, in a camp – it's a very nomadic-type camp. I live with my parents; we travel from bazaar to bazaar and they sell things.

'When I'm ten, my parents and others are slaughtered by a band of men. The men take me with them and I am eventually sold to be trained as a dancer. I later meet a woman who takes me from the theatre and educates and helps me. She then puts me into a household, a real house of a man, a sheikh. I feel really grateful and good about this. I live in a harem with the other wives. It's a very comfortable life. There are ten of us. I have a son and he is very loving.

'I see myself living to be very old and when I die I am surrounded by people. I die a happy woman.'

To return to the subject of having been a different gender, of course many of the gay men I have taken back in time have not been surprised to find they were women last time around. Maybe that explains some of their desires to cross dress. In fact, I regressed a boy recently who came up as a very glamorous female, a sort of *femme fatale* type, and when he described her to me he was absolutely amazed and went very quiet for a while, but later explained that when he dresses in drag he always has this very clear image of one type of woman in his mind and now he knows he is actually recreating himself in a former life!

I had the opportunity to regress the American female impersonator Jim Bailey when he was doing a concert at the London Palladium. He is famous in the States for his on-the-nose impression of Judy Garland – in fact he does a whole show as Judy which is quite remarkable. He also impersonates Barbra Streisand, Peggy Lee and the marvellous Phyllis Diller. His show, which he calls *An Intimate Evening with Judy Garland,* is not to be missed. After seeing it, you feel as though you have just seen her in the flesh. So it was not too much of a surprise that he should see a life as a woman.

> 'I'm in a smoke-filled room; it's cigarette smoke. There's a lot of green felt tables, sort of pool or roulette tables – it's like some sort of nightclub. There's only one other person there: a man wearing a white shirt and black pants, a black vest and has two black garters on his arms and a Derby hat on his head. He has a black moustache and sideburns and black eyes. As I'm looking at him he seems elevated; he looks like he's posing. I don't get warmth from this man; he's not smiling. I'm a woman and I've got very white skin and am wearing white. I've got long, dark ash blonde hair, wavy and parted in the middle. I'm wearing a plain, flowing caftan that comes to a vee in the middle. I'm in my twenties and am trying to help this man somehow. I don't feel right in this club. I'm misplaced. There's no one else around, just him and me.'

We go back to her childhood.

> 'I feel it's way before the 1920s. I live in a grey
> place with lots of pipes and a grey draped bed. I'm
> about ten years old and I'm out playing in the
> garden. I'm wearing white boots like patent leather
> with white stockings and a white dress with blonde
> hair worn in two braids. I'm waiting for my parents
> who are coming up the road. Mother is in white
> and she's laughing. Father is the same guy I was
> with in the nightclub earlier, only this time he's
> wearing a grey outfit and hat. It must be the late
> 1800s because he's got a grey Ascot on.'

We return to the nightclub scene.

> 'He's doing something illegal and I'm trying to stop
> him. I'm also there to say goodbye as I'm leaving in
> the morning by boat. Mother has gone now. I can
> see myself on the boat now, It's like a ferry and it
> takes me to an island with lots of green trees.
> There's no sign of life as the boat approaches. We
> dock at a dark, wooden place, a sort of boathouse;
> there's lots of other boats there. Someone finally
> comes to meet me: an older man in shirt sleeves.
> He takes my luggage and we go off in a carriage to
> a house with stained glass windows, a nice house. I
> think we are in America. There's lots of light and
> windows in the house.
>
> 'By the time I'm thirty-five, I've red-dyed hair
> and am very made up, I'm sitting at a table with a
> glass of red wine. My dress is beautiful in white
> lace. I seem to own this place. Later I'm desperately
> trying to find something – I feel I've hidden some
> money and can't find it. A man comes into the
> room but I don't want him to know I'm looking
> for something.

'Six months later I'm in hospital; I tried to commit suicide. I don't know why – I think I did it to get some attention. I slit my wrists. I'm still alone; I always seem to be alone.

'One year later I'm in a place with lots of people. It seems as though it's Europe and I'm walking down a road. It's a festive sort of thing and everyone's wearing evening clothes. My hair is red and beautifully dressed; I'm wearing pearl earrings and necklace and a dress with a bustle. Later I'm at a hotel with a man and woman; the man has a moustache and grey hair – he's older and wears a cape. I feel it's my sister and her husband.

'I later go to work in some sort of factory or shop. I'm very stern and well past fifty. I'm an instructress of some kind. It could even be a school, I can't tell.

'I die as I lived, alone. I have grey hair. I feel as I go to the light that I am re-united with my father.'

The room seemed heavy with depression after this life so I whisked into his next session post-haste.

'I'm a man this time. I live in a red brick house with a black fence around it – there are several in the block. I'm in my thirties and it's my house. I work in some sort of office and I walk to it every day, very formally dressed. It's the 1900s, I think. I'm something to do with shipping things – there are lots of crates with statues in them.'

We go back to the age of ten.

'Father is a very stern man and is away a lot. He has a moustache. Mother is very happy but I'm not a very happy child.'

We move on to the age of sixty.

> 'I'm in an old-fashioned car but I can't figure out
> how to start it. I've done very well for myself. I've
> got two children and my marriage worked out well.
> I was very old when I was finally taken ill. I
> managed to get home and get to bed. I died happy
> and felt I'd achieved happiness.'

I felt I had to whisk him through the second life because I
knew nothing unusual had happened in it but I just wanted
him to be left with the glow of that very secure and contented
memory.

Talking about it later, Jim felt he'd had to deal with being
alone in the first regression. He's alone in this present life and
says he likes it that way, but in the past he's found it very hard.
He said, 'I've always felt I may wind up being alone at the end
of my life but I know I can deal with it now.'

I have found that it's not just gender and colour that
leaves a lasting impression on us but places we have lived
before. Many of my clients see lives they have lived in other
countries, and generally if it was a happy life they have a deep
love and feeling for the place – and, of course, vice versa. For
example, Elton John has a passion for Paris and says it has a
smell for him that he feels he knows. Other people who have
moved from abroad to live in Britain trace their love of this
country back to being happy here in a past life.

Elton John's ex-wife Renate is one of these people. She
was born and grew up in Germany but says she was obsessed
with England from when she was a small child. She learned
to speak English at an early age and speaks with scarcely a
trace of a German accent. So, of course, we were not surprised
to find she had had a couple of lives in Britain. She did
laughingly say that she hoped she would not come up as Eva
Braun! Her sessions were very enjoyable as we did them on
my boat with the water gently lapping up against the sides and

Renate being lulled happily into four past lives on the trot.

'I'm looking at an old hand. I'm wearing
comfortable black slippers, a dark, shapeless skirt
hanging to the ankles and a dark, long-sleeved
shapeless top. Looking in the mirror I can see the
face of a seventy year old woman. My bedroom is
very tidy with nothing much in it but it's very light.
Through the window I can see flowers, roses and
countryside. Opposite the bedroom is the kitchen
with an Aga-style range and a wooden table. There
is a man in there who is my son.

'I must have been here all my life because at
the age of six I'm in the same place.

'At fifteen I'm outside on a bicycle but not
going to school but to work. It's dusty where my
father works, with lots of machinery – wheels and
knives – and a lot of other people are working
there too. It's a big room with sacks in it. I work
here delivering: I take things in the basket on my
bicycle and deliver them. I don't know whether I
have any brothers or sisters but my father is dressed
in baggy beige trousers and a beige cap. I can't read!

'I'm twenty now and working in a garden all
alone, digging and weeding. My closest friend is a
dog. I can't remember my mother; she's dead and
someone else looks after me. By the time I'm
twenty-five I'm delivering on the bike again. I'm
quite content because I don't know any different.

'Around thirty I get married. I can see a party
outside: it's not dressy, everyone's loud and boozy.
Looks like a farming community, but I don't
recognise the country. Later I work with wood –
I'm chopping wood.

'I'm around fifty now and my son is around
somewhere. There's a trauma. My husband drinks –

someone has just told me he is dead, he had an accident whilst drunk. Ten years later I'm going deaf; all I do is mend and knit. At the end I'm in bed all alone.'

Renate was still trapped in the bed so I took her to the light and then gently led her into the next memory.

'I've a man's hand and I'm holding a candle. The clothes are of a coarse material; I can't see the cut but I'm wearing sandals. I'm standing in front of a church tower. The entrance is a heavy door pointed at the top; it's a stone building. I'm in a small, cold, damp room. The main part of the church is high and cold. It's not decorated except for the windows. The altar is very plain.

'I'm back in the little ante-room picking up robes to give to someone: there's a man I can see who puts them on. They're different from mine – white and purple – he is the priest. I take care of the place and ring the bells. I live near the church with my wife and kids but I'm not very happy. I'm happiest in the little ante-room.

'I'm about forty but my wife is much younger than me. I can see her: she has long dark hair and is wearing a long brown skirt. I suppose she could be Italian. There are a lot of olive trees around. I don't think I'm particularly dedicated. I became the warden by following in my family footsteps. But I'm envious of the priest because I would like to do the services. I would like to be the priest so perhaps there is dedication. I know most of the congregation and feel I'm related to the priest somehow.

'Something seems to have gone wrong with my life because I've run away from the church and my wife and I don't want ever to go back there. My last memory is of running down the steps of the bell tower and out as quickly as possible, desperately trying to get away. I run straight round to my mother's but I can't talk to her. I can't talk to anyone. I'm very confused.'

Can't you go to the priest?

'He isn't there any more. I can't go back to the church, I can't ever go to any church again!'

Let's face what happened, let's look at it together.

'I followed the priest up the stairs to the bell tower. I am really jealous of him – I'd like to be a priest. I've pushed him off the tower! I've murdered him.
      'I'm running for a long time, many months, I'm following the road. I'm in despair – it's very grim. I've found a job on a farm and am staying there working in the fields for the rest of my time. One day I'm taken ill in the field. It's raining, they put me in a horse-drawn cart to take me for help but I die passing through some woods.'

Again she stays trapped in the cart and we go into the light and clear the whole thing away. It took me a long time to get her to see what she did there. I had to keep taking her back and back again until finally she seemed to want to get the whole thing off her chest and blurted out what had happened. I am probably the first person she has ever told of this thing in all those lives. Renate did at first decide not to have this printed but later decided to print and be damned! She then went straight into the first of her English lives.

'I'm seeing an oak-panelled door. The room is dark, it's very big and ornate, and there are pictures in gold frames. Perhaps it's a ballroom. There's not much furniture but it's all ornate, gold and red. I can't see any windows. I'm wearing Mozart-style shoes like carpet slippers. I'm in men's clothes: the trousers end below the knee, my stockings and jacket are the same greyish-white colour all in the same Mozart style and I've got a ruffled neck tie. I'm wearing a big ring on my finger. In the mirror the face I can see is of a man in his late forties or early fifties wearing a powdered wig. I have horrible eyes that bulge: bulbous sticky-out eyes.

'Outside there are hedges and a park. I think I'm dressed up for some kind of party. People are arriving and I'm standing by the door serving drinks and taking coats. I have a cramped little room at the top of a small staircase; it's wood-panelled. I have quite an interesting life. In the kitchen there are a lot of gossipy women.'

We go back to ten years old.

'I'm on a farm with happy and understanding parents. I go to the village school, but the kids always make fun of my eyes. I'm used to it so I don't feel too bad about it. There's no uniforms – we all wear different things, but we're poor.'

We go forward to the first day at work.

'In the kitchen of the big house someone is talking to me. I'm taken to a room, I put my case down and then I'm shown round the place and explained what I'm supposed to do. I think I'm going to be serving meals. I also take care of the ornate carriages. I'm taken to the big hall to see the owners. The woman is really quite bossy and in charge. I don't like her – she's quite hard to please and a social climber. The husband is quite sweet and chubby, he's obviously very wealthy; they're some kind of blue-bloods.'

We return to the point where she first came in.

'I'm standing sorting carriages out and cloaks and hats as the guests are all leaving. The lady of the house is standing there, I think she's angry with me although she's being very pleasant to the people still there. I don't know what's happened but I'm sent packing. I'm coming down the stairs alone carrying my case.'

I take Renate to the last moment of this life as she can't seem to see anything more. For quite a while she can only see a tiled floor and everything seems very dark. I take this situation into a light and she finally sees what happened.

'I've committed suicide, I'm hanging from the ceiling.'

This, of course, had to be taken to the light and we finally cleared it away. In the last two lives her mind had blocked the trauma of what she had done wrong and although we found the information eventually in the first one, we couldn't get there in the second one, but we are looking at both of them having gone terribly wrong.

'There's a front door with one of those little porches to keep the rain out – a little house with a lovely feeling about it, very cosy and homely. It's crammed full of things: dried flowers, lots of books, very messy. I'm wearing a cardigan, check shirt, thick stockings, flat shoes and I'm about sixty. It's my house and I've got cats and I'm very happy. In the evening friends, all about my age, come around and we play cards; there's two couples and a couple of women.'

We go back ten years.

'I'm married to a man who's wearing a uniform – his best uniform – it looks like a pilot or perhaps a captain. I don't know what nationality he is.'

We go back to when she was a little girl.

'I'm hanging the washing out for my mother. I'm happy. I meet my husband at school. The wedding is a bit of a let-down. I expected a lot from it but it's a bit of a boring party. My husband is in uniform, he's a regular serviceman. We have one boy and one girl, and it's a fulfilling marriage, very cheerful. He's away a lot of the time, but it's no problem, I'm very happy. The little boy looks exactly like my brother did (in this life): he's very cute with the same hairstyle and a gap in his teeth. As he gets older he becomes very mischievous but I can't stay mad at him for long. He marries an old girlfriend who I don't get on with very well, so I don't see a lot of him any more. I don't see my daughter much either but she was never as important to me as the boy was.'

We go the very end of the life.

'I'm in church, kneeling and praying. I go outside and slip and fall – it's the beginning of my end. I'm in a hospital bed.'

She went straight to the light this time and I was very

pleased that at last we got a happy life. I felt that perhaps the son was her brother in this life as they are very close now. I couldn't hold her in the light and bring forward the son because the session had been too long and I felt I was fading in power.

Later on we discussed the lives and she felt sure the last two were England, and perhaps even the first one, too. I really liked the last little old lady as she felt such a comfortable and satisfied person. Renate also went away feeling very well and slept really well for the first time in ages. I suppose it's marvellous to get so much off one's mind in one fell swoop!

Renate and I have remained very good friends as we have so much in common in our marriages – in fact, we call ourselves the Ex-wives Club! There are more of us, too: Cynthia Lennon and Maureen Starr were very much like us and I see quite a lot of Mary Austin, Freddie Mercury's ex-girlfriend to whom he left his whole estate. Maybe one day we will have EXW reunion dinners with dish (dish as in gossip!) as the main dish. Who would not wish to be a fly on the wall on these occasions? We are all haunted by budding biographers who want the real story of our marriages. I expect they'd give their right arm to be there.

I once regressed a very famous actress, who decided at the very last moment to remain anonymous, who also seemed to go to her spiritual home in her regression. I went out to her country home to do this session and what a wonderful place it is, with a thatched roof and a beautiful lake – the perfect place for a peaceful sitting. Interestingly enough, we were joined for the whole session by her cat, who seemed to love the power expressed during the sitting. All animals love to get near the healing power – my own pets revel in it. However, everything did not go quite smoothly as when I got home I found the tape was blank and I had to write the regression from my memory. This is very difficult as my mind is so far away during the regression. However, here's all I could recall.

She came in by a stone building constructed with different-sized stones. It felt really old and had a big wooden door. When she went inside it felt surprisingly warm. She saw herself as a woman with brown hair and bare feet, with a very weathered brown face and hands, aged about forty. She seemed to be carting heavy packages from place to place, bundles wrapped up in cloth rather like Dick Whittington's belongings. She was a travelling woman, a sort of nomad.

I took her back to the age of twenty to find out more. She was living in a brick-built house dressed very formally in a high-waisted blue dress. By the look of the scene she was quite well off. She had her own bedroom which was very charmingly decorated and furnished. She belonged to a large family, one of about four children. There were also lots of pets, cats and dogs, a very happy home.

Perhaps, I thought at the time, that was why her cat had wanted to sit in.

She was sent overseas to attend a Catholic college where she learned French, Latin and needlework. She then saw herself leaving the college and was greatly relieved as she hated being there. She was taken in a trap to a market place where she changed to another horse-drawn buggy that took her to a small dock. From there she transferred to a boat where there were lots of different families, all huddled together and seemingly in great distress. They finally reached their destination to find there was no one to meet her, so she had to wait around with the unhappy families. After a long time fruitlessly waiting she eventually tramped off with them to find her own family.

She arrived at her village to find it had been under siege and her whole family had perished. She saw rocks being rolled out and down the hill on to people. She ended up making her escape and taking two small just-orphaned children with her. She travelled for weeks and weeks with them doing odd farm work and anything they could get to keep alive. Finally they reached a convent and the nuns took the children in. The nuns had blue habits and grey headdresses. She was then alone and met an old couple who gave her lodgings for a while, but she was forced to spend her life travelling and living any way she could.

She grew accustomed to her nomadic life and lived to a ripe old age. She died in some sort of building where the people put her out on a ledge so she could see the magnificence of the countryside and the open sea. When I took her to the light she looked back and felt that this life taught her how to survive and be alone.

Later she said she knew it was Scotland and told me that she now visits there often and feels she has second sight when she's there. She also said she felt all her lines meet there but just hasn't found the right location yet. The whole experience left her feeling wonderful.

❖

CHAPTER SEVEN

We'll Meet Again

I mentioned earlier that smells are often prominent in regressions and you may remember the client I talked about at the beginning of this book who thought she smelled awful. Another case that I have never forgotten was a lady who came to me to help her deal with a marriage that was falling apart. We had had quite a few counselling sessions and she finally admitted to me that she had been too embarrassed to tell me that every time her husband came towards her to make love to her, she sensed a most foul smell of what she could only describe as stale sex and blood. This gave me a clue as to what may be going wrong, as I have mentioned before that people have to come together again in lives when there is what we call karmic debt – a debt accrued in a previous incarnation, which illustrates the old sayings 'what goes round comes round' and 'you reap what you sow'. When we got together for her next appointment, I put the client into a past time.

> She saw herself as a young American Indian sitting outside her tepee. There appeared to be only women in the camp, so the men must have been away on a hunting trip or something. Suddenly they were attacked by a gang of white men who ran amok amongst the women. In terror, she ran

into the woods in a desperate attempt to escape but was caught by one man who raped her viciously and then mutilated her with his knife, cutting off her breasts and leaving her to die. As she recalled that death, she still felt as though she were lying there in the undergrowth.

She was literally trapped in her fear. I released the poor soul into the light and left her there to clear the vision, but as she went towards the light she saw again quite clearly the face of the man who had murdered her. To her amazement his face blurred and reformed and she found herself looking into the familiar face of her husband!

She never experienced that smell again, and understood why the physical side of her relationship with her husband had always revolted her. She had always thought that she was sexually inadequate. She did say, though, that her ample breasts had been what first attracted her husband to her. I don't know how this debt will be worked out but I'm sure it will. They have a wonderful family in this life and things have been much better since she saw that life. I suppose she has forgiven him.

I did come across a few celebrities who saw their present partner in their past-life memories. One of these was Janet Reger, the renowned lingerie designer. Another was Brian May from the rock group Queen.

Most women would be very happy to be given an exclusive item of sexy silk underwear designed and hand-made for the Janet Reger label. I, for one, have spent dream-time gazing at her creations in her Knightsbridge salon! So it was with joyful anticipation that I waited for her to come along to my home for her regressions. She did not disappoint me. She is a lady of great depth of character, and very interesting company, a woman who has had her share of grief and joy. I felt that if she had not ended up helping women in their bedrooms with her alluring designs, she would have made a very good counsellor and been able to help women in their trials of life, although perhaps she has been more help in solving marital problems in the career she did choose! She saw two lives on that day and they were very clear and precise, so I have reproduced them in her own words.

'I can see an eye: it's darkish grey and small. I'm in a courtyard which is paved and there's a lot of plants and bushes, especially towards the end, and there's a door there made of glass like a French window. The plants are not like English plants, they're very brightly coloured and lush dark greens. The door leads to a room with a stripped, polished wood floor with blue and green rugs. It's sort of Regency or Georgian furniture, very highly polished wooden pieces and lots of flowers and books. The room looks quite English but then again the flowers don't. The books are written in a strange script, like Greek or Russian, those sort of letters – I can't read it!

'I'm wearing cloth slippers, very ugly old-fashioned ones with clumsy-looking toes and a little flap on them, red with yellowy brown plaid. I've got quite big feet. I'm wearing thick beige stockings; I don't like them. I've a long white cotton apron on that ties at the back. It looks like a maid's apron, it's not frilly but very plain and there's a beige and black skirt underneath. The blouse is black and my hair is grey. I think I'm in my sixties. I sleep right at the top of the house. I'm now standing at the bottom of the staircase and I'm having difficulty getting myself to go up the stairs. I don't want to go up there.

I have to coax her to her room.

'It's very dark. I don't like this place. There's

someone else in the room, it's a woman. I can see her eyes, they're the same eyes that I first saw, but I could see only one then. I feel uneasy about this woman. She doesn't mind me being there, but I mind her being there, even though I know she belongs there. I'm a maid and she's one too, I just don't like her. I was already working at the house when she came. She was quite young and I feel that she is pushing me out. She quite likes me but I'll never like her because she makes me feel insecure. I feel everybody's going to like her more than me – it's a sort of childish feeling. I was also quite young when she first came but I'm jealous of her.'

I take her back to age ten.

'I can see an isolated cottage with a rather overgrown garden. My parents are wearing clogs, they look like a Bruegel painting, they must be Dutch. They're not elegant. Dad's wearing a brown jacket thing with straight trousers and clogs. They're very nice people. He works outside in the garden and grows things and looks after the chickens; it's a sort of small farm.

'When I was old enough to work I was sent to the live-in job at the house I'm still at. I work for a family: they're all quite grown up, there aren't any small children there. My job is to keep things tidy and clean – I work in the kitchen a lot and I also do all the fireplaces. I don't enjoy it, I'd rather be at home. I do like the family, but I envy them. They don't do a lot; they go out often and organise parties and entertain. They all look so nice, they all look good. I don't go out much, I don't have a very good life there at all. The girl I dislike shares my room. I hate it.

'At the end of my life I'm in a hospital. I'm in a big ward with simple beds. The nurse is wearing a long striped dress with a pinny over the top. I feel very bad, I'm very old and very tired. I die alone, except for the others in the ward. I felt I wasted that life.'

As that life cleared away, we went straight into the second of her memories, so here it is, again in her own words.

'I'm outdoors in a big open space quite a long way away. I can see some small shabby houses and I'm going towards them. I'm in Europe. I feel I've travelled here, but I live somewhere else. I'm nicely dressed in a long robe with a corded belt round my waist and a veil-like thing over my hair which has a little thing holding it on top of my head. It's in medieval style, roundish, with my hair flowing around it loose. I'm about seventeen years old and I'm riding a big brown horse with a fringed saddle. I'm meeting someone, a man I really like. He's about twenty and he's wearing trousers and a top in brown with a tunic and belt; he's also got a chain around his neck. He has longish hair and he lives nearby and has ridden to this spot to meet me. His house is beautiful – it's like a castle that is quite a way from the main village. It's not a normal castle, it's white, not a heavy building, but with lots of little points and decorative things on the roof. I've never seen a building like this before, it's more like a Loire château but much smaller.

'I live in another town a long way away from here. Our house is made of stone and quite nice. My father is a soldier. We all eat at a long dark table dotted with blue painted bowls. There's fruit and a grain cereal in milk, some sort of baked pudding. Mother's wearing a very loose, long dress with long pointed sleeves. She looks nice and slim. The kitchen is very primitive: it's sort of outside the house with just a little roof over it. I thought I was in England but I'm not so sure now. There's a plump girl working in the kitchen with a big open fire with a huge black pot over it. It's just where I feel there ought to be an outside wall, but there isn't one. The smoke is going out into the grounds. She's stirring the pot with a big, flat piece of wood, it's not scooped out like a spoon. I don't do a lot; I ride sometimes and mother tells me stories. We don't see a lot of dad. I think he's angry with me – everybody seems to be angry with me in this life. I think I'm quite difficult. They all want me to be something else.

'I met the boy when he visited my home town. He's a soldier too, and we met in the street. He knew someone I was with and we stopped and talked. I later ran away from home to live with him. I'm now seeing myself a few years later, I'm in a bedroom lying on the bed. There's a lot of red in the room and a red cover over the bed. I'm dying. I've been through some traumatic situation with this man. I feel he's to blame for my death – he didn't kill me but it's his fault. I became very ill but I didn't realise I was dying, I thought I'd get better. I love him but I have become hysterically ill and weak and unable to cope. I feel he hasn't looked after me properly. He says he loves me, but he doesn't love me the way I want to be loved. I became very unhappy and stopped eating and made myself very seriously ill. I blame him.'

As I took Janet into the light to clear this death, she again saw her soldier boy as a much older man coming in to be reunited with her, but as she looked into his face the image faded and changed into the face of her husband in this lifetime. Sadly, he committed suicide a few years earlier. She told me she had been told that she had been with him in earlier lives before seeing this, and was thrilled to have been shown where, as she had always thought that perhaps she had been his mother.

She felt her hatred of housework and dreary clothes were a hangover from the first life she saw. I must admit to having had to smile, whilst conducting this particular session, at the tone of her voice in which she described the slippers and other garments, which displayed utter horror and disgust! Perhaps the memory of that life spurred on her desire to dress as many women as she could in silks and lace. In the second life she felt she had learned to love as she gave herself totally to her husband. I can't comment on why things went wrong this time around, but I believe that it can often take many lifetimes to build unconditional love, and feel sure things must have been learned by each of them now to have moved them nearer their goal.

The session I did with Brian May proved particularly difficult simply because of his busy schedule. I had known Brian since the band Queen first came into the public eye. The night they completed their first huge hit 'Bohemian Rhapsody' they were so pleased with the session that the whole group rushed out to the home I shared with my former husband, Kenny Everett, in the Cotswolds and played it to us. I had also asked Freddie Mercury to sit for this book, and at one point – in a haze of Champagne – he had said yes, but later in the cold light of day he had declared himself far too afraid even to consider it.

Brian, however, is a braver boy and so we made our arrangements and decided that to get this in the bag as soon as possible I would meet him at his office whilst he was in town and fit it in with other things he had to do there. Not the best situation to say the least, as I generally do my work in such sheltered conditions, but after that particular session I feel I could probably work in the midst of war! Mind you, that reminds me of one very bizarre request I received while I was working on the book. After my successful sitting with Jimmy Tarbuck, he had told a few friends how much he had enjoyed it and I received a phone call from the boxer Henry Cooper asking me if I could do one with him on the telephone! Bless him. Anyway, Brian and I got together in the sitting room above the Queen office in Notting Hill Gate amidst non-stop ringing telephones, buses almost passing my ear and people buzzing about busily with not a care for the fact that I was to take Brian time-travelling. That we managed to get back to any memory at all I felt was nothing short of a miracle. I'll once more print the regression as it happened, but with all the stoppages, interruptions and my words neatly edited out.

'I'm seeing a very light reddish coloured wooden door with two large panels at the top and two smaller below. As I reach out my hand to open the door I see that it's a bit more hairy than my present hand. I'm wearing a tweedy jacket and brown trousers with black, shiny, pointed shoes. Inside the room there are pictures on the wall with gilt frames, mostly landscapes. It's a big sitting room with sofas and lots of people all standing around drinking cocktails. They are all dressed quite smartly, smarter than I am. I think I'm just visiting. I realise now it's a funeral I'm attending.

'I live in an end of terrace house in the early twentieth century. The dining room has quite a big table. There's a lady sitting there with slightly greying hair, a gentle lady. I'm quite old; I feel she's my wife. There's just her and me now – it feels like everyone else has gone.'

We hold it there and go back to when he was just fifteen years old.

> 'I live in a big house and my parents are quite jolly-looking. Dad's wearing a brown suit with a fob watch. It feels like 1860. I think my dad is a photographer. My first job is working outside on a farm, where there are pigs and cows. I don't like it very much. I feel like I want to get away.
>
> 'By the time I'm twenty I'm an apprenticed to what seems to be a solicitor – I'm learning a trade.
>
> 'I get married at what looks like Clapham Common: it's a church on a big green. I can't see the wife though.'

I take him to the altar.

> 'I can see her now: she's very beautiful, soft and warm. She's very young, about eighteen, but very beautiful with a straight nose. Our first married home seems to be the terraced house I first saw.
>
> 'By the time I'm thirty we have three children. I'm still at the same job in the city at the same office. I think I'm a solicitor or something.'

He goes to fifty years old.

> 'I'm in the small house in the study, sitting behind a desk. I've received a piece of paper that tells me what's happening. Someone has died and they are a long way away, in India or somewhere. I don't know who it is because I can't sort of feel anything. It feels like it's professionally important. A year later we are living in the big house; we moved into it after the news of the death of my business partner. It feels big and empty and I don't feel I've

enough furniture to fill it. I feel we didn't want to move out of our lovely terraced house.'

We return to where we came in at the funeral. Whose funeral is it?

'I realise now it's my own. I'm seeing it all, looking at all the guests, it's very strange.'

We go into the light where he is rejoined by his beloved wife, looking the same age as when he died. She suddenly fades and changes. He goes very quiet. I ask him who he is looking at now.

'It's Anita, she now looks like Anita.'

The actress Anita Dobson is his long-time partner in this life. After we closed that life I attempted to put him into another life, but he kept returning to the same one, which made me realise that he was so connected to it that he had obviously something to work out this time. He was quite pleased to see this life as it explained his passion for collecting photographs of that same era and with his father being a professional photographer of that time this obsession now seems to have a basis.

Brian commented how overwhelmingly sad he was at his own funeral, not because he had died, but because he was leaving his wife. It looks like his desire not to be parted from her has carried through to this life, too.

The actor Anton Rodgers contacted me a long time ago because he was interested in seeing into his past, but time kept passing us by until finally we got together in London to go time-travelling. (I have since moved to the country and am a near neighbour of his now.) He's a very spiritual man and already has firm beliefs of his own, so I am very happy to include him in this project. He turned out to be another person who saw someone in this life from his past. We saw three lives in quick succession.

'There's a children's story-type door with six panels and it's drawn by an artist and there's no wall either side. I can see a light through the door and I'm standing in a field of poppies. It's as if I'm on an enormous high hill in Switzerland. (It's like *The Sound of Music*.) I've gone through the door now and am sitting in a chair by one of those old stoves in the kitchen. It's an iron stove, it's very Laurentian (D. H. Lawrence mining type). It's a small kitchen and I suppose it's in the twenties. I'm about forty and am wearing a shirt with no collar, boots and corduroy trousers. Ugh! I'm smoking a pipe!

'It's like a mine worker's cottage with a back yard, a terraced house most definitely English. Inside there's a thin little staircase with just two rooms upstairs; my room has just got enough room for a double bed. I'm married to a woman with curlers in her hair; she's wearing a heavy flannelette nightie. I work in a mill. I'm in charge of a lathe that makes cotton. (I did a play set in a mill about a year ago.) It's been a happy life but everything's not well at present. I live in fear of my wife's illness. I'm worried about her because she's dying and she doesn't know it. She actually died shortly after this time and I spent my life grieving for her.

'At my death I'm seeing myself joining up with her again; it's very light where we are. She just can't believe we are together again, it's enormously peaceful. She's telling me she's pleased that I've stopped smoking. The wife is beginning to fade now and she is coming back into focus again – she has turned into my mother in this life!'

Anton told me later that he had lost his mother a short while ago, but when she was alive he was extremely close to her. There was a very warm glow in the room when he saw her. One of the loveliest parts of my work is that I get to share in some wonderful moments. When they occur the air in the room seems to go very still, like time has stopped – it's almost tangible. We sat in the stillness of that reunion for a short while, then moved on to the next life.

> 'I'm seeing the staircase from that film *A Matter of Life and Death* – it had an enormous effect on me because the staircase was going up to heaven.'

I felt this was a hangover from his warm glow, so pushed him forward.

> 'I'm in a street in a village. It's terrifically beautiful, pastoral English, a bright sunny day. It's as if the world is at peace. I can feel the heat, it's so warm and sunny. It's about four in the afternoon. I'm looking for something – I don't belong here. I'm at a gate with a sort of gable over it which leads to a low thatched cottage. A woman answers the door – she's got grey hair in a bun. She's wearing a blue dress to the floor with a little roll collar and an apron on top. It's about 1860. I'm wearing nice white shoes, rather like cricket shoes. I'm very tall with a blazer and a straw hat. I'm about eighteen years old. I've come to the cottage to see the woman's husband; he's one of my family's servants. He's been ill and I'm enquiring how he is.
>
> 'I live in an enormous house. It's like Bath, the West Country. It's rather like *Brideshead Revisited*. We eat in a large room at a big table. I sit down, stage left. My mother is sitting by me wearing a twenties outfit: a beautiful long, low-waisted dress.

Father's at the other end of the table: he's an older man. I love him very much. He owns the whole thing. He earned his money himself and owns many things. I'm still at school – the clothes I'm wearing are the school uniform, the blazer in red, blue and white stripes, just like the cricket clothes.

'At twenty-one I'm in the trenches. I'm an officer in France. I've got bands on my feet. I've no helmet on. I'm killed in the trenches. Everything's gone into slow motion.'

We went into silence again to clear the situation then headed straight for life three.

'I'm in Italy on a mountain. I'm a herdsman wearing very tough clothing, like leather, and I'm tending goats. I'm about forty years old. I live in a wooden house, sort of like William Tell. I'm married with two children and we're quite happy.

'By the age of fifty I'm a village leader. I'm asked my opinion a lot. I'm sort of happy with this position but I realise it's superficial happiness because the real power lies with the landed gentry and we don't have any at all really. I get very angry that it's so unfair and there's nothing anyone can do about it. I don't work for them, I'm very independent, but in terms of trying to achieve anything for the people in the village it's all in the hands of the gentry and they do nothing – they couldn't care less.

'At the age of sixty I find myself sitting in the village café and I'm bitter, it's all been a waste.

'At the very end of my life I'm surrounded by family. I'm lying on my bed dying but nobody seems to care – they've gone off me because of my bitterness. I'm above my body and I'm looking at myself and know I'm dying and I'm thinking:

thank God, now I can start again. As I die I see myself as a sort of Icarus (the man with wax-and-feather wings who flew too near the sun, causing his wings to melt). I'm saying I don't care a shit if my wings melt – who cares, at least I tried. It's as a result of that life's bitterness.'

Anton said afterwards:
'That was fascinating. It was all as if they were clips from films, sort of dream-like. I suppose that's what dreams are. I've had a theory all my life about time. I feel we've lived this life already and what we're experiencing is the reflection of it and as we go forward, so we look further back and that's why we get déjà vu. If we could only look far enough we could see our deaths.

'The image I saw of the tables and chairs, I saw recently when I read a script about tables and chairs and I envisaged the ones I saw just then, so I suppose that's us visualising things that are already in our far memory.

'I have a recurring dream full of joy and see a spaceship hovering in the sky. Then a while ago I saw the film *Close Encounters* and I was amazed because it was the same thing as in my dream. I believe Stephen Spielberg has the link.'

Anton also told me he felt a link in this life to his death in the trenches. When he had been eleven years old in the Second World War, he lived in London in Chester Square. In the air raids the family slept under the stairs in the cellar, and when the buzz bombs came over he used to scream in terror. His sisters always managed to make him laugh and brought him out of his fears – they were not afraid like him. I was also a war child in Sheffield where we were bombed heavily because we lived near the munitions factories, but I never felt fear. I only feared for my cat if we couldn't find her, and for my father who was out fighting the fires. It was only Anton's far memory that gave him his terror. He felt the other link was that in this life he has this terrible fear of being a phoney because his tastes and his attitude to life are moneyed but yet he didn't come from a wealthy background. His taste is also totally Victorian and late Georgian and the grand house he lived in was Georgian. He found this incredible. He felt as I do that one's tastes are determined by the memories that come from ones happiest times, and they could have been any time back in history.

His last comment was that he could still see himself looking down at his herdsman's body and thinking, 'I've wasted that life, I'll never do that again.'

Another unusual client case in this category of reunions was a lovely lady singer-songwriter who is very spiritual and quite psychic. She came to me to develop her gifts in the healing field. After being with me for a short while she asked me if I could regress her for reasons that she did not, at first, wish to reveal to me. We had the session and it really was most unusual in the fact that the first place she saw she told me she knew really well. At first I thought she had gone back in her present life but that was not the case, as I will explain after I relay the regression as it happened.

> She saw an ancient croft on a remote Scottish island with earth floor and just one room as the complete living quarters. She was a young lady with one child. She found herself to be a widow having been married to a fisherman who had lost his life at sea. It was a very hard existence. She later found a man washed up on the shore from a shipwreck and discovered that he was from one of the ships belonging to the Spanish Armada. She felt sorry for him and took him to a place she knew to hide him, as he would have been killed by her kinsmen as the country was at war with Spain. She nursed him back to health, but while she was caring for him they fell madly in love with each other. Then one day she caught a very bad cold out on the cliffs and died suddenly.

She did not go to the light so I went through the usual procedure and tried to get her there. She could see the light but I could not get her to go towards it. I persisted, as usual, and got her there to find that she was still very unhappy. She told me she was worried about her Spaniard. I decided to bring the time forward to his own death and bring him into the light to join her, thus clearing her of this sadness. When her lover came into the light, I let him fade and reform and asked who he looked like now and she replied,

'My present partner.'

At the end of the session she explained that she had almost finished writing a novel about this same life. She had been living with her present partner for a few years and ever since they linked up she had been seeing the croft house and quite extensive flashes of the complete life. She told me that her partner had also seen the life, too, but the unusual aspect of this was that he looked almost exactly the same in this incarnation while she looked completely different. The one trouble was that they were both experiencing deep periods of sudden and inexplicable depression. This, of course, was because they had not gone to the light and were frequently tuning into the tragedy of the past. She left me feeling very weepy, which is not usual at all, but she was upset because she felt that I had taken her past self away from her forever. Later that day she popped back and left the following letter with my assistant.

'Dear Lee,
In meditation after I saw you this morning, I saw my mother (she died last year). I asked her if she would welcome and take care of Meggie (the woman from the Scottish island) and she said she would. Meggie also came to me in meditation. She was smiling, laughing in fact, dancing and singing,

none of which I have ever visualised or "seen" her do before. She was very happy indeed and said to me that I did not need to sit with her in that room any more and that I was free to get up and get on with my own life. The whole thing is rather like shedding a skin and I feel a bit strange but it's not an unpleasant feeling. I have cried a few times for Meggie, but they are as much tears of joy as they are tears of sadness. She's so familiar to me; she's just in another place now. Thank you for helping me to release her into the light and in doing so, release me too.'

I have mentioned before that it is interesting to regress someone who is psychic and this is a very good example. She even had the memory of which island it was, and on researching found it true that there had been a wreckage of a Spanish ship off the very shore. I feel that the story she writes about that life will be a wonderful love story. It made me wonder how many other novels are simply someone reliving a long-past memory!

I know that to people who have never even thought of past lives as a reality, the last few reunions may seem pretty far-fetched, but in my daily life they are quite a common occurrence, and when you think that out of about thirty celebrity memories that I have up to this point completed for this book, three out of that thirty have met up with old friends again, this shows that it is not that unusual.

After the first proof of my own long-gone past, I was told by the lady who regressed me that my then husband, Kenny Everett, had been my own child in two past incarnations. I'm sort of sad to say that after being shown about ten of my past lives, I still haven't been shown any of these particular ones as proof to me of this fact. But instinctively, I feel that it is true, as in our marriage in this life I played out a very mothering role, as that is how my behaviour was led by my emotions. I have always been ruled by my heart and have never been able to go against it. At the time I was informed of the mother/son theory, I was having a particularly miserable time and couldn't understand why I stuck around. But when I was told this, it made me view the whole situation differently and instead of wallowing in self-pity, I dissected the circumstances and was left with the feeling that I was only there to mother him once more through that period of his life. The knowledge being given to me at that time gave me the strength and determination to complete that task. In fact, since being made aware that there is this reason for every deep liaison, I have conducted my life in a much calmer state – which if you had ever read the story of what has happened to me already, says a hell of a lot.

The more I look back at what happened with Kenny, the more I think that perhaps we all volunteer to come to each other's lives at certain points just to assist in one particular way, a way that perhaps has been successful before. From where I'm viewing life, who's to say we don't all gather at the beginning of a loved one's incarnation to work out how we can all appear and help! All I know is I'm not in any way afraid of death. I'm not being the slightest bit morbid but I look forward to it because I feel that when it comes I'll have finished the stint I volunteered for this time. In the same way I try very hard to make as good a job of whatever crisis that is placed before me with the thought that I must get it right this time so that I don't have to re-do it next time.

Before I end this chapter of heavenly reunions, I must tell you about a young man of about twenty-five who had travelled to us from his homeland of Australia. He was referred to me by a counsellor who felt that regression could help to solve this boy's problems. The boy had fled his home because he was experiencing feelings that filled him with horror. He had had a best friend at school with whom he was extremely close. He was quite happy with their relationship until in their twenties his friend had met and fallen in love with a girl. The boy could not believe his reaction to the situation. He became extremely jealous and began to experience feelings of love for his friend; he desired him. He tried all sorts of ways to split up his friend from his girlfriend. Had he been homosexual, the feelings would have been normal, but in this young man they made him feel so disgusted that he packed up and not only left his home but his country, too. He had come to England to hide. He said he never had any feelings for any other men and felt he couldn't live with these alien emotions.

When I regressed him, he came up in a life where he was a normal, happy man who married a lovely woman and lived a full happy life with her and their children. When he died, he couldn't bear to be parted from her and I had to force him to the light out of his favourite leather chair on which he had decided to stay.

I got him to the light and brought his wife in and – yes, you've guessed it – she turned into his best friend in this life. At last he understood why he had been tormented by such strange feelings. He returned to his country feeling that with this new understanding he could at last deal with the situation.

He would naturally have carried forward this great love for his friend into this life, but because his spirit from that life had not been cleared he had still retained the feelings of a man for a woman. When I am able to help someone in that way it makes me realise that even when I feel jaded, I know my work must carry on, so that more can be understood about it. I'll die a happier person if past-life clearance work becomes a normal and everyday occurrence.

Yesterday I had an experience that I just had to add to this chapter. It seems so relevant and so weird that I can't even begin to give an explanation of it. I had regressed the Australian actor Simon Burke, and he had relived a life in which he had married and lived quite happily to the end of the life. After we had closed the session he kept exclaiming that he had seen his wife's face so clearly that it had shocked him and he could still see her in his mind. He had left my consultancy with my autobiography in his hand to read on the tube journey home. That night I received this fax message from him.

'Dear Lee,
Something rather strange and wonderful happened straight after seeing you which I thought you might like to hear about. I was on the tube going home and opened up your book and became engrossed in your prologue. After about fifteen minutes, a girl next to me said in a kind of East-End voice, "So who's it about then? I've been reading a page over your shoulder." Now no-one speaks to me ever EVER on the tube and I didn't like it. I glanced at her short tarty skirt and handbag and said to her rather gruffly to put her off, "Her name is Lee Everett, she's a spiritual healer; she used to be married to Kenny Everett." "So she's been about a bit then has she?" I tried to get on with reading your book and then something told me to look at her face. I did and yes, it was the girl I had just seen with you in my head, the bride. A bit scruffier, a few freckles, but unmistakably that girl.
　'It was my stop so I got up and left the train feeling very light-headed. As it moved off I turned to see if she was looking at me. As the train gathered speed, her carriage passed and she was looking at me with a small, knowing kind of reassuring smile. What the hell do you make of that?!!!'

As I said earlier, I can't shed any light on it at all but it certainly was some sort of reunion that left us all feeling rather like we had witnessed something out of a weird movie. Life and lives certainly are stranger than fiction.

CHAPTER EIGHT

❖

The Ones That
Got Away

I am always being asked whether everyone can be regressed or if I have a lot of failures. Well, it's extremely rare in my consultancy to find someone who cannot be regressed. Sometimes the subject can be very difficult, but I'm so experienced that I have never given up. It gets easier and easier as the years roll by because with practice I become a better practitioner. Years ago when I had just started working in the field, it took me much longer, but the power does build up with confidence.

Sometimes the client goes back to a time in this present life that needs to be examined and cleared – another aspect of regression. For example, a journalist came to me for an interview and she explained that she had an overwhelming fear of birds. I took her into her childhood and she saw herself in her pram being wheeled into someone's lounge. Her mother then went into the kitchen with her friend and a large parrot flew from his perch and landed on her pram, causing her to scream hysterically. Another time a young man came to me from New Zealand. He had one of the worst stutters I've ever come across. He felt it must have come from a past life as he had been like that as long as he could remember. When I put him back he saw himself as a toddler crawling around the floor. He had been left with his grandfather whilst his mother was out. He was in exuberant mood and making a lot of noise, when suddenly his grandfather cracked and grabbed the child and shook him viciously. This made him immediately go quiet and from that time on he associated speech with that shaking. His stutter did not miraculously disappear, but he kept in touch and it did gradually improve.

I do think, though, that because my clients come to me seeking to be taken back that I am always working with willing subjects. Regressing the celebrities was very different as I had approached them – which meant that it was not always so easy. I did have two failures amongst those I contacted; strangely enough both of them well-known eccentrics. The first one was a long-time favourite of mine, Spike Milligan. I had – like thousands of others – been a Goon Show fanatic, and the off-the-wall humour he has shown throughout his career has always held me. In fact my ex-husband Kenny had him as a guest one morning on his breakfast radio show and Spike turned up in his pyjamas! `

I was thrilled when Spike agreed to sit for me, and I travelled down to his home town on the Sussex coast the night before. I travelled through the countryside and down winding lanes to reach his house and was let in by the great man himself. I followed him into his lounge and my mouth fell open when I found myself looking at a view of the sea that seemed to stretch to eternity. What a wonderful home. We talked for ages about life, the world and everything, then we settled down to work.

Well, let's say I settled down! It was like trying to hold on to something I couldn't see. His mind is so like a butterfly dashing here there and everywhere, it was impossible to keep his concentration. We both felt that it was to do with the fact that he is a manic depressive. He has had hypnosis in the past and I felt that he would have progressed better under hypnosis again. He did agree to try it that way but we never got around to finding the right practitioner. He did go in to the right state a few times, but his mind always jolted him back. He also went easily back to his early childhood to when he remembers

being happiest. I have transcribed the tape so you can read for
yourself what a hard time I had, but perhaps also understand
him a little more. I have left in a little more of my own
questions in this regression than in earlier ones to help you
understand how the process works.

> 'I can see a hall; it's the hall I left about five minutes
> ago.'

Can you find a door?

> 'It's the door of the baptistry in Florence, they
> denote biblical and scenes from life. The staircase
> has a stair carpet with brass polished Victorian rods
> across it. It's the one I used to live in called
> Monkey Rest, a Victorian House. I lived in it about
> two years ago!
>
> 'This is the door of my childhood home. It
> opens on to a flagstone path going off to the right.
> Immediately in front of me there's a glass beaded
> curtain with cream, blue and gold glass. I'm about
> six or seven.'

At that moment, the door bell rang.

> 'There's a buzzing here!'

It's the door. Were you happy then?

> 'I don't know if I was happy, I think I was
> sensitive. I don't know whether I was happy or
> ever meant to be happy.'

Is there a door?

> 'It's the same door. I'm six or seven.'

Is there a staircase?

> 'Same staircase, I'm afraid, the one at Monkey Rest
> with the red stair carpet.'

Were you happy there?

'Yes I was, there was sadness in the house at times but I was very much in love, but with the buildings I've described. I think you'll find it difficult for me to move out of these images because I was very much a person who wanted to stay in one place forever. I wanted to stay in the house I described to you, as a child. I wanted to stay in Monkey Rest forever! We moved when I was nearly nine to Rangoon in Burma and went to a house there. I don't particularly remember being happy.'

I took him back to the age of six.

'I was a solitary child, an only child. It was a matriarchal house, my father was always away. After that the most powerful comes my grandmother; I found her the most kind and gentle. I think to this day I loved her more than my own mother. I feel I can still see her very clearly indeed and hear her voice, very quiet. I feel her non-stop, it's so powerful. I can't shake off my yesterdays at all, they are overwhelming. As I get older I live in terrible sadness. It's not that I've got older, it's just that that time has gone.'

It's not really gone, it's in the memory, like money in the bank.

'I wish sometimes I could just switch them off because they're laden with nostalgic sadness. I think the reason is that I live in such a manic depressive twilight now that anything rather than now is preferential and the past is the only thing I know that was secure. We're stuck in the present and the future's unknown and the future as I see it is nauseating.'

I have faith in what there is. See light, visualise a window.

'It's a window with blue sky outside, that's all. It's a square window that opens outwards with wooden frames and clasps to hold it open against the wind. It's not attached to any walls, it's just floating in space.'

What can you see through it?

'Just sky. I'm trying to make it have sea as well but it's just a blankish nothing at all really.'

Can you see in through the window?

'It's rather red. I think the sunlight's shining on part of a red carpet; the table and chairs are wooden, I can't see what period they are. On the left-hand side there's a Welsh dresser in dark wood. I can't see anything else.'

What's the room like?

'My natural assumption is that there would be a fireplace at the other end somewhere. I can't see it though, it's like the room doesn't exist at the right-hand side, there's darkness.'

Turn the light on.

'There's nothing much at all. There might be a bench. I think I'm resisting seeing anything there.'

Are you afraid?

'No, not really, no.' (suddenly) 'I'll have to draw this to a close in a minute because a man's come to see me, can I continue it? I'll have to see this man.'

Spike left the room at that point as though he were afraid. On his return he couldn't even conjure light so I talked to him until he could see the window again.

'Okay, it's a very misty window. It's not straight, it's

at an angle; it's a sash window. Now it's disappeared, it's not happening, I've got very thin eyelids and what I'm seeing are the floaters in my eyes. I'll cut the light out if I can.' He clutched his eyes tightly. 'It's just blank. I'm not very helpful am I?'

Would you rather not do this?

'No, I'd like to go along with you.'

Can you see a light?

'I keep seeing a spotlight on a stage. It's a painting by Serle, a couple dancing in a spotlight and I did a drawing of it, it's Victorian. That's what I can see.'

Bask in the light, sunbathe. Can you see a staircase?

'It's the staircase at Kensington Palace, the one down which I believe Queen Victoria came in a nightdress to announce the fact she was Queen, about 1830. I'm not there though. There were two people came to tell her, Lord Somebody and Lord and Lady So and So. I saw it as if I was standing on it looking down. I've actually seen it physically and in paintings.'

Don't think, follow your memory.

'Oh that's easy. I can't see a door. It's a blank.'

I try a parachute jump method. Sometimes if the sitter is very difficult I get them to imagine they are in an aeroplane and have them jump with a parachute and get them to float slowly downwards through the sunlight above the clouds and very slowly and gently down to the earth. By the time they have felt the flow of the floating motion it generally has relaxed them and made the mind go quiet.

'I can see a church with a steeple, a Victorian one. It keeps getting superimposed by a domed one like

St Paul's. I haven't landed yet, I'm still looking
down on it. It's the countryside. It's all gone now.
I'm nowhere.'

I take him on a wander.

'I'm seeing a stone staircase inside a tower going
upwards, a circular staircase.'

Can you see your feet?

'I've got black shoes with a buckle on, they're
Jacobean shoes. Knowing that Jacobean legs have
white stockings, I'm inventing them. It's all gone
blank again now.'

I get him back to a door.

'It's lying on it's side. It has a huge painting of
Christ painted on it. The door's sideways. It's a
door with panels with Christ painted on from top
to bottom but it's faded away now. It was suspended
in space. It's like I'm sitting up high somehow.'

On a building?

'A long, tall column. It could be Nelson's. It's like
ghostly white suspended in darkness, I can see the
top. It's gone now and I'm seeing nothing at all.
    'My mind's wandering, I'm afraid, to the De la
Warr Pavilion where we are having a reunion soon
and I'm worried about the electric lights – it's a
fuse that's not been replaced.'

You are butterflying.

'I can't help it.'

Let's try once more. Try and go back before your memory was
damaged.

'Nothing's very clear. There's a faint ghost of what

looks like a mirror with gilt around it, now it's gone.'

Bring back the bench you saw earlier.

'I know there's a bench there but it's all dark now.'

I'll light it up.

'I can't see it, Lee, it's all blank. There was a bench there a while back but it's all gone blank now. I remember the chairs and table but it's all very ghostly and I can't really see it, Lee.'

Have you ever had hypnosis?

'Yes, I did very well. It was for a sleep problem; it solved it at the time. I had to lay down and stare at a red light on the ceiling. I'd start to get drowsy and get a feeling of well-being and relaxation and all the tension flowed from me and gradually I'd feel very sleepy and my eyelids would start to shut and they'd get heavier and heavier and flicker and flicker and maybe my eyes would close and it would be a blessed relief and I'd go into a deep, tranquil sleep. I still use it but it's often too difficult so I have to take tablets.'

Try self-hypnosis.

'I'm seeing a lighthouse. I'm up in the sky looking down on it. Now I can't see the light, it's all black and a strange blue glow, but that's gone now. I think it's just an optical illusion affecting the lens of my eyes somehow. It's coming from inside not outside.'

Colour is healing, I tell Spike. Colours have positive vibrations, like yellow in spring.

'Yes, colour must have vibrations. Blackbirds only choose the yellow crocuses to eat.'

I talk to him about colour and how it is used for healing and that he should try to visualise light in colour to bathe in.

'I'd like to but I can't see the light. I don't think I'm a very good subject, Lee.'

No, you aren't, Spike. Let's close now.

'I wasn't very good, was I? I hope I'm not a disappointment to you, Lee.'

I tried to explain that he should not think like that, and we talked for ages about faith and my beliefs, healing and strengthening. I told him I wished I could help him, bless him.

Just writing that again has made me feel so sad. Every time the images went dark meant his mind had come forward again. He had brain damage from the war when he was injured by shrapnel and noise attack. I'm afraid I would have had to have worked with him a long time before getting anywhere at all. I still think that his sitting gives a wonderful insight into the terrible suffering Spike and many other ex-soldiers still endure, being manic depressive from a wound like his cannot be treated in the same way as a normal depression would be, and even the specialists can't really be of much help. My heart went out to him that day and I think a little part of it will always be his. A truly sensitive, caring loving man, he has mass love from his fans but still nothing can help him. The only thing that helps me cope with this is that I know there is a reason for everything and somehow his life will eventually yield more than we or he can see, and only time will show him that.

On reflection, there have been other forms of failure in the work I have done – or perhaps it is wrong to call them failure, they were just very different. They occurred about fifteen years ago and showed a pattern I have not yet fathomed, nor do I think I need to yet. Two people came to me for regression, both were terminally ill. I know you will probably say that I am a healer so why could I not heal them.

I never know when anyone is to be healed as I never let my mind become involved, but even if there is not complete healing, there is always great help given. In the two cases I'm about to relate I had been helping them get ready to die. I had been counselling those closest to them and making them strong for the events to follow. They both, at separate times, asked me to regress them and I agreed.

The outcome was very strange. In both cases, they did not regress, but went into the future! One of them saw a space age existence with very weird modes of transport, and the other, a younger man, saw a life in New York that was very modern, very futuristic – and the weird thing about it was he has never been to America. I cannot explain this; but it sure does make you think, doesn't it?

The second celebrity whose regression was a semi-failure was the Marquis of Bath, Alexander Thynne. He was very difficult to regress as he is a bit deaf and I generally speak in dulcet tones, but had to speak up and I felt that broke the spell a little. I have known the Marquis for some time now. In fact, I have spent time as his guest at Longleat House. He is one of my favourite eccentrics: he always makes me laugh, is very witty and his lifestyle is utterly unique. He wears no shoes, has long hair tied back, and has many, what he calls 'wifelets'.

The first time we met, my husband, John, and I were invited with a friend of ours to spend the weekend with him, and he gave us a wing of Longleat in which to stay. We thought it was to be an intimate weekend with just himself and his latest wifelet of that time, Jo Jo Laine. Jo Jo is the ex-wife of Denny Laine, the musician who was originally part of the band Procol Harum and later played with Paul and Linda McCartney. I had known her for some time and she wanted Alexander to meet us. Because we only expected a small gathering of friends, we thought dinner would be a cosy little meal. But we dressed for dinner and went along to the dining room to find it full of women of varying colours. John thought it was a United Nations meeting, but we later found out they were all wifelets and had emerged from their respective cottages in the grounds. At dinner I felt I was in a real-life soap! We soon found out why the press have named him the Loins of Longleat! We did, however, have a marvellous time as he is a great host.

At lunch, the following day, we all crowded around the table and opposite me sat a rather large man. As he lowered himself on to his chair it completely collapsed and shattered into pieces. It was really funny to see him disappear from sight. The butler, Cuthbert, came in and removed the debris and replaced the man – unhurt apart from his pride – on a much sterner seat. To break the ice, someone commented, 'Oh there goes a Chippendale' to which the Marquis calmly replied, 'Sheraton actually'. Never a dull moment.

Alexander didn't really want to be regressed but did it just to please me. In fact, when I rang him one day at Longleat to set a date to do this session, he said he had just been discussing the regression but he called it 'recession'. I finally did the regression at his London flat, which is always in disarray because he paints there and does his writing there, too. He has a habit of having a day bed: at Longleat it's a sixties mock fur chaise longue but in London it's just a mattress on the floor. So for this session he was laid out on his floor day bed and I had to manoeuvre a microphone and myself as near to him as possible, not an easy task at all. Anyway it didn't really happen but this is how it went, and it needed lots of questioning from me to keep the session moving. We started by my asking him to visualise a door.

> **'Can you speak up a bit? The trouble with that is I might be visualising a door at Longleat! It's a door with a marble frame, wooden door with inset pattern. I'm in the little breakfast room at Longleat.'**

We move away.

> **'There's a green door with a brass handle the wall**

is white, it's an inside door. Inside I think it goes off to the left; it's a longer depth. I might have been coming from another room before that. It's a gymnasium, it has a wooden planked floor. I have bare feet. I'm assuming they are my feet. It's like my preparatory school – it's a linoleum floored corridor. Down the corridor leads to a kitchen, a Victorian kitchen, it's similar to a Victorian kitchen with copper things on walls and jars and a kitchen table with cooking on a large scale – boilings and simmerings, various things on the stove, a Victorian stove. The whole time I'm linking too much to images formed at Longleat.'

There is a show kitchen at Longleat exactly as he described here. Are there people in the kitchen?

'They are in clothes that I would associate with a Victorian kitchen – cloth and cotton caps and aprons etc. – with I would think rabbit cooking.'

Again, this is just like the show place.

'I'm not escaping from Longleat imagery.'

I close this down and we go quiet and try again.

'There's a staircase with quite a significant banister going up three times to a little passage or a thing up on top, a rather heavily square banister.'

Do you know this banister?

'I don't think I do. It has a wooden floor and large sized staircase. I go up five steps and it has a platform, then up another again. It could be that there is armoury on the walls, shields with some weapons. I feel a hand stretch out to hold the banister. It might have a lace cuff, Van Dyke style; it's a man's hand. I'm now going into a Van Dyke picture sort of association. The shoes could have a buckle on them, black shoes, in general. I fear I'm slipping back into Longleat imagery again.'

Stick to the staircase.

'There's a bit of a passage up to a narrower staircase, then small passages around. I can't escape from Longleat.'

You wouldn't be wearing that kind of costume there would you?

'It's quite conceivable that I would!'

We laugh, and I point out that he has shoes on – as he rarely does in this life!

'Ah I think it's only the twenty-first century that we shed them. Every time I leave my mind blank to suggestion, the suggestion comes that it's a Longleat scene. I escape it but then it comes back. Like if you say let's make a word, the actual bricks you're giving me to make a word are in a pack called Longleat.'

That's your mind coming in again. We try and clear everything away yet again.

'I'm in the open and I'm looking out over a quite flat panoramic vista with woodland and fields, hedged fields. It's relatively high land. I'm not aware of any buildings.'

Let's walk. Look at your feet, are you wearing shoes?

'Yes boots, leather, quite high, no, average height, I suppose. I've got a cottage door with ivy on it – a very old door. It might be a shed, it's something like a woodshed but nobody's in there. They are men's boots, and I'm wearing a leather jerkin with baggy sleeves. I'm in a large white house, maybe a tiled roof, maybe Spanish-type arches with windows behind the sort of terraces and balustrades.'

Go in. Have you seen this place before?

'I'm sure it must be suggested by many images I've seen but nothing I'm specifically aware of (thank God). I'm up in the balustrades going into what probably would be a bedroom. I'm not seeing anyone there. It's a Spanish sort of scene. I can't specifically identify the furniture to what I know to be Spanish, it's more the wooden kind of stuff.'

Do you know this bedroom?

'No, I've more a feeling of walking round it and seeing it and it's in considerable disarray, so its not as I would expect it to be. Now I'm in a room that I'm assuming is the kitchen. Tiled floor of different colours, a wood-burning stove, sideboard, washing sinks and a table. I feel I'm viewing it all rather than participating in it. I wouldn't associate it with eating – that's probably in the dining room of this house. There is again a wide-sleeved kind of outfit with black and white colours with some bright red flowers and some patches of colour. There's a violin being played, probably just some stringed instruments, probably playing Vivaldi-type music.'

We go to the dining room to see where he would sit and eat.

'I'm on the side – I think I'm a guest. I'm bewigged with black moustache. I cannot feel my hands are any different to my own hands. I'm still in leather jerkin and puffed sleeves. Maybe the trousers are like plus fours and I think I still have boots on. There's a family at the table with some young ones.

'The sitting room is carpeted. I've got a feeling of it being more French in style here, Louis XIV kind of furniture.'

Where would you sleep?

'The idea was that when I was over the balustrade that I was going to see the bedroom, but I found it in a state of total disarray – someone had rifled it or sacked it. Someone had been there but wasn't there then – it was not as I would expect to find it.'

Let's see the room before it was sacked.

'Four-poster bed, large pillars and velvet up top. I'm always viewing. I've not yet seen the person in it, I'm just there on my own.'

What's in the clothes closet?

'Capes, largely. I think I'm younger now, maybe the groom's son visiting, rather from a similar large house.'

The groom's son? Isn't it something you wanted to be in this life – ordinary?

'Maybe, it doesn't really relate.'

Let's see the groom's house.

'Maybe it was the cottage adjoining. I'm not getting anywhere you know.'

You have seen quite a lot and it's all around the same period.

'The trouble is I see things then some pieces come in like a painting and I'm back at Longleat. I'm not feeling spontaneous.'

Maybe we should have tried you with a hypnotist?

'Oh yes, and then I won't have the inabilities of my own life, but I don't think I could be hypnotised either.'

I suppose it is difficult when someone lives in a stately home and sort of museum like Longleat, as it is almost like living in a kind of regression. I know we had a small success when he began seeing the groom's son, but I don't feel he wanted to be involved with them. The room in disarray was interesting as in a normal sitting that would probably have been a key part of the life and I would have been able to do a bit of detective work and discover more. Still, never mind eh?

I suppose while I am looking at the ones that got away I should say that I have a mass of letters of refusal tucked away in a file. I could about put a book together on the actual hard work it was in getting my subjects to agree. I had a delightful letter from Victoria Wood, for example, saying that she had enough trouble with this life and couldn't cope with any more! I even still have ones who agreed to sit for me and we still haven't found a time to do them yet. Peter Stringfellow and Zandra Rhodes are just two, but I'm pleased to report that most of them replied. I just have to mention one celebrity in particular, though, Christine Keeler – the girl who shot to fame in the Profumo scandal as one of the call girls involved. Her representative contacted me and said that Christine would sit for me but I would have to pay a huge fee! Some people don't change do they?

CHAPTER NINE

❖

Unconditional Love

From all my work in this field I have realised that the power of love is the most powerful force in the world. It is the light. So it appears that while we are in an incarnation we are either trying to build on the loves that have already begun in the past, or beginning a completely new love. There have been many examples of this in our celebrities. Janet Reger, the lingerie designer, was a very good illustration. She had had two previous liaisons with her present husband and even this one ended badly, but each time there seems to have been a different lesson. When Brian May first met Anita Dobson in this lifetime, they had experienced an instant attraction, a feeling that it was the right thing. When I met Kenny Everett in this time we became inseparable. Even before I left my then partner Billy Fury, Ev would be at our house at weekends and he would often just follow me around as though his life depended on me. When we eventually became lovers we saw a strange light surround us that felt enormously powerful. Even on one occasion after we had begun fighting and had separated, we met for lunch to agree who should live where. We had started the meeting in acrimony but whilst in mid-meal that damn light appeared and he ended up coming back to our house again with me. We had many false starts before we finally did split up. But as I had been told I was his mother in two past lives and I see the mothering I did in this last life, it really does make sense. I wonder how we'll relate to each other next time.

When he was alive he used to pooh-pooh most of the things I did, but that is not what he felt deep down as he often sent people to see me on a professional basis. It was just something he couldn't fight. He was jealous of my work in the way that he couldn't share it so resented it. In fact, my personal assistant had made an appointment with a very good medium three weeks before he died unexpectedly. She had wanted to have a reading for her birthday but the medium in practice had been on his holidays and could not give her an appointment until just over three weeks later; that date fell two days after Ev passed into spirit!

When she went for her session to this medium, who did not know her or know that she worked with me, her session was taken up with what the medium called a very insistent comical person who would not leave him alone and called himself Maurice Cole. That's Ev's real name; mine is Audrey. We used to have a message on our answerphone that said: 'This is Maurice and Audrey singing for you'. Even our wedding invitations said: 'Maurice and Audrey invite you . . .'. He insisted on leaving a message for me and called me mother and said he really knew I had been before now as he could see the plot for himself! Much more was said at this first contact that proved to me that it was totally genuine. Strangely enough, now that I have had more communication with him he calls me his wife. What with having contact with Billy Fury, too, who also calls me his wife, my husband John feels he's in some kind of club himself!

With John I have always felt that he was brought forward in my life at a time when I was to have total support in my work. He had already developed as a healer years before and he understands my work and the effect it has upon me. We have been shown lives together in the past, too. One was when I was his mother in Italy: he was a scholar and very successful and we had been devoted to each other. Another life was as

Native Americans and he was my brave, I was his squaw. In the numerous communications I have had with the other side they have always referred to him as my brave! He was Running Bear, an Indian scout. He still runs to this day – in fact his best way of relaxing is to run for miles and miles. I believe we had achieved unconditional love in the past and he has been brought to me to make my work easier. Even though I worked right through the painful break up with Ev, it really used to take its toll. Now I work with no marital emotions to cope with and no insecurity – we both have total faith in each other. Believe me, that's rare for me, as I've never known it before, apart from with my parents.

So it seems to me that throughout our lives people are brought to us at certain times to help us achieve what we came for. I think that nothing is wasted, even though many people feel that when they split up with someone life is ruined forever. Not so – the love that was made can never fade. Only the end result of a lesson goes with a soul memory, so it makes sense that every time we meet again we add to this love. I always loved the line in the Beatles song 'The love you make is equal to the love you take' and it is so very true. I hear so many people in my consulting room say that since they have left someone they have realised what they did wrong and wish they could make a fresh start, but of course they can.

I have often counselled families who have lost a baby, a loss that has changed their whole lives. When anyone loses a little one I see it as the child having just touched the earth, coming to bring about the change in the lives it affected. Maybe that spirit of the child volunteered to come to the earth for the short stay just to help in bringing about their loved ones' progress. I always feel that everything in life is put there for us to overcome. Anyone who has suffered tragedy will tell you that in retrospect they find that the event has brought about many positive things. The pain is to be welcomed in life as it supplies the growth. I find Michael Jackson a good case in point as he has spent most of his life suffering and the music he brings forward is very spiritual. I feel he is a channel when he writes, as are many of our songwriters. Being channels does not, of course, make them saints; they are here to live their own lives and grow too.

I can honestly look back on some of the worst things that have happened to me – and there have been many – and know that if it weren't for those things I wouldn't have achieved what I have. I'm grateful for all the pain. It is hard to look at it that way when you're in the midst of the horror, but I manage always to tell myself that I will see the reason for what is happening in due course and it makes things easier to bear. Everything I have suffered has given me empathy with my clients; I have gone through similar experiences and can feel their pain with them. I look at life's traumas as a rough sea and as you would in heavy waters I lie still and just keep afloat. I never listen to my mind in these times as that seems to be the thing that takes the worst knocks. In lying still, I mean I keep my mind quiet and try to find something to occupy myself until we reach the shore. In fact, suffering to me is like having an injection: if you relax it doesn't hurt. In the same way, I seem to go through things painlessly because I understand and always manage to keep my faith throughout it all.

I had a marvellous lady in my consulting room last year who had had a very serious cancer and had almost died. I was helping her with her recovery and we spent a lot of time discussing the effect her illness had had upon her immediate family. The whole family had been pulled together in their fear of losing her. A daughter who she had not even been speaking to had realised how much she loved her mother and had come to her side in a stronger way than ever before, and the rest of her family, too.

Knowing that there is no death does not make me able to shake off grief altogether because there is always the physical loss to get over. I think everyone should grieve properly and get it out of their system, but the knowledge that loved ones are still there and will be there for us when we pass over makes the grief shorter. I always see my grief as a bit selfish in that it is just for me alone, as I know the lost one is in a place I will be so pleased to go to when this life is completed, so I have the conflict of being pleased for them and trying not to hold them in sadness of my loss. Anyway life is very short and we never have a long wait before these reunions.

I have a picture in my mind that has formed through my experience in my work, that perhaps when we are about to leave the spirit world for our next incarnation all our loved ones gather around and work out what role they can play in our new life. I also know that we are all guided and helped along our path. I feel that when the parts to play in our life are handed out, some of those who love us stay up in the light as guides. I feel that when we are up in the light – or at home as I like to see it – we look at our past experiences and failures and decide which thing to go into the physical to achieve or get right this time. The powerful love between the guide and the life forms the bridge across the divide and it's always there for us, only the darkness that comes into the mind makes us feel alone, but we are never really alone.

I see the physical as a maze of life, through which our guides can show us the easiest, quickest way, giving us instructions at the right time, if we are listening. The way to keep listening is to try and keep as bright as possible by not letting the mind clutter and chatter on about nothing, especially negative things. I know that as long as I remember to try and keep my mind on light thoughts like happy and positive things, then I am still able to hear my inner directions. I often see people walking down the road with a terrible scowl on their face, even though it is a lovely day. They are probably thinking things that are totally unnecessary and have got so accustomed to letting their minds work on their own that they are not even conscious that they are thinking at all. It's a bad habit that most of us humans get into. I always watch my mind and replace any persistently negative thoughts with happy memories or plans. If I am worrying about making a decision, then I make it, knowing that I can change my mind later if necessary. In a way, I meditate most of the day, keeping my mind for when its needed for practical tasks like drawing up a shopping list. I never hold on to a hurt or an insult – that only makes you tired and ill. Remember that there is a bigger justice that will put things right in the end. Revenge only creates another wrong to be put right. That is the law of karma, cause and effect.

I often see clients who say that they cannot possibly be helped by a loved one as they don't know anyone who has passed into spirit and have no love at all; they feel they don't even know what love is. But even if you cannot remember a past, it is there and in that past there will be many loves and many helpers. Again in the words of The Beatles, 'The love you make is equal to the love you take', and that is it in a nutshell. Never close your heart if you have been hurt, for fear of being hurt again. Do go on and love again and again if need be; you must never stop trying. You can see all around you the faces of people who have closed their hearts; there is no light there, no spark and their lives are not happy at all. That's why regression often helps because they feel the power of love and that can give them back their hope and make their path through life more even.

Don't let petty things stop you achieving what you all volunteered to come and do, or you'll get back home at the end of it all only to find you went all the way there and didn't do it and will probably have to come all the way back and do it again. I'm taking no risks. I stick my neck out, follow my instincts and get involved with everything that comes my way. I love many people in this life with me. I don't force myself to try to love everybody as that would be ignoring my guidance. There are some people that we should not get involved with on our path and if I have an aversion to someone I don't try and work out why I don't like that person, I just know it's my instincts telling me that that person is not for me, not in my path. If I forced myself – like many good

Christians will tell you to do – I know that I will be wasting their time and they mine. In fact, if you force yourself to go against your natural instincts then you will actually be off your path and hold the person concerned off theirs, too. Life is too short to waste.

The more my life goes on, the more sure I am that my faith is right. I have a strong bond of love with others in my field, and with many clients, both in this life and in the light, many of whom come to speak as well as the ones I have sought out. Who knows that in lives to come they will come back as helpers.

I told you early on in this book of the life as a nun who was badly tortured in the Spanish Inquisition, but I only told you a small part of it. Years after that regression when I had a consultancy in Bayswater called The House of Spirit, I was holding a group one evening that consisted of nine girls that I felt had a gift and were developing towards the healing field. We were a very close bunch as all my groups become. We held the group each week at the same time. I arrived later than usual on this particular night as I had been on hospital visits. When I arrived my PA came to meet me in the hall with a sheepish look on her face. She told me that a blind man had come to our door, saying that he had heard a voice that told him to find me as I would be his healer, and he had said that his voice had guided him to where I was! The group nights are very private and separate from my consultancies and they are also absent healing sessions, so I was quite annoyed that she had shown this man into my group room, but I had no choice but to go in. When I saw him I was amazed as he had so many things wrong with him that I felt I would not know where to start to heal him. As I walked into the room silently and began settling in, he called across the room to me, 'It's Lee, isn't it?' so I had to go across to him, but I still could not shake this feeling of not wanting to see him, which was so alien to my thoughts at work. I put my hand on him and spoke, but immediately welled up into tears; emotion racked my whole body. I just could not fathom the extent of my feelings about this man.

Anyway, time passed on until it was almost time to begin our group and I couldn't throw him out on to the street so asked the girls if they would mind if this man joined us for the evening, something that had never happened before or since. They were fascinated and eagerly agreed. I suppose they thought they could practise their healing on him. I asked him what he felt I could heal as he was riddled with afflictions, and he said he had been told I would heal his soul! I told him he could join us in meditating, and he explained that he had practised meditation most of his life as he had been born clairvoyant. So we sat as usual and had a powerful session.

Afterwards I asked him to tell us all about himself – and what a catalogue of horror it was. He had knocked his toe as a young boy and the injury was so severe that he ended up losing the whole toe, then later he had fallen from a ladder and broken his leg (the other leg) so badly that he was left with one leg shorter than the other. He had a list of other things that had happened internally and left all manner of problems including incontinence at a very young age. He had had an infection in the left eye that had taken his sight and then glaucoma in the other eye, causing him to lose the sight of that eye too. He looked as though he had been in a war. In short, at separate times he had had every bone in his body broken.

I still felt strange about him. I usually feel great love come through when I'm about to give healing; it's generally brought forward by the ones who love the subject in spirit and goes through me, but this time I had no sympathy – well not at first – and could not understand why I felt like this. When I went and put my hands on him I had the strangest surge of a power I could not identify and with this surge I saw quite clearly in my inner vision the Spanish soldier that I had seen in the nun regression who had tortured me in the dungeon. I asked him if he had ever been shown a life in Spain and he immediately told me that he had been my torturer and fell into my arms sobbing and asking my forgiveness. I automatically told him that there was nothing to forgive and he said that that was the healing he had been sent to receive. By this time all my girls were in tears and the tissues were being passed around like sweets.

The other interesting thing that happened was that at the same time as I saw the soldier, I also saw one of the nuns who had betrayed us all. She was in the room with us in this life, and she also had a physical disability. I never told anyone about that part – not her or any of them – but I know she saw the same thing as I saw because there came about a great change in her after that. I know this must seem very far-fetched to the layman but I had ten witnesses. One of those girls was a journalist called Ellen Petrie who has since married Dereck Jameson (a wedding I really enjoyed) and they both now have their own popular radio show on the BBC. Mind you, Ellen witnessed many incredible things around that time and has since become a very good astrologer.

That last episode to my nun's life was an amazing event for me as I never thought that I would be confronted with my torturer, the very man who broke every bone in my body a few hundred years ago. (Mind who you hurt in future!) In a way, he is in my life now and obviously this lifetime was his time of retribution – I hope he has paid his debts now and next time will come back with a clean slate. It may seem strange to include this episode in a chapter on unconditional love, but even though he and I met in such horrendous circumstances, his lives and mine are now intertwined and I like to think that it could be the beginning of another love. After all, love has to start somewhere and we have now a small but potent history together.

I believe the power of love can even give a kind of life to inanimate objects. I have many belongings that I cherish and feel have a character. I can walk around my home and feel many emotions from my collections of things. Many of them have been given to me by people I love and most of them have a history. I have already set them out in a will to make sure that these things will continue to be loved. In fact, I think of them as I would a pet and feel they have to be cared for to the best of my ability. I have many crystals that are great examples of power-holders. Some of them are millions of years old, and in the same way that a building can soak up experiences that occur within its walls, these crystals have been in the earth throughout most of its experiences and they have been many past incarnations. I have a shop in London that specialises in collectors' pieces of crystal and mineral. We find that the people who collect them see them as entities, and the healing power of these stones has long been known.

Collectors also give these crystals as gifts – wonderful and powerful presents – although it is common knowledge that a stolen crystal will bring the thief very bad luck. This was proved to me a few years ago. I had a robbery at my consultancy and a whole cabinet of crystals was taken. A few weeks later one of the culprits returned a huge holdall containing all the stolen crystals to the police station. Apart from my CD collection these were the only things recovered. The thief who stole them is now languishing in jail and the stones are back where they belong. The robbery involved at least three people but he was the only one caught!

Just last week my assistant opened our shop as usual to find a short note dropped through the letter box. It said, 'Please find a basket of crystals behind the flower box – made homeless'. There, sure enough, was a waste paper basket full of beautiful crystals, all carefully and individually wrapped. It was rather like finding a baby on the doorstep. If the past owner of these stones ever reads this they will be pleased to know that I have put them into my private collection and feel I am only fostering them until they are reclaimed. But the point of this is that I feel not only do human beings have a soul memory that contains their whole past but so do land sites, buildings and even inanimate objects. There are some people who practise psychometry, which is the art of holding an object and then telling you all about the owner. This done by an expert can be quite uncanny – and demonstrates that the object has a feeling all of its own.

I have in this life rescued many animals. When I was living with Billy we had a bird rescue sanctuary and had as many as five hundred birds at any one time, not to mention dogs, cats and other animals. I feel every time we use the power of our love on some animal, that also is the beginning of another love link. I remember one time seeing a rabbit in my head-lights whilst driving home one night. I stopped and literally had to scrape him off the road, his back half was totally squashed – it was horrendous. I rushed him home and gave him brandy and water in a syringe and he slowly fell asleep. I felt he would just drift off into spirit as he slept very deeply. I finally went to bed but in the middle of the night I actually saw this rabbit in my sleep floating upwards and looking straight at me. The vision was so clear that I got up and rushed downstairs to find he had passed on and obviously had only that last minute gone as he was still warm and soft. I felt he had popped in to say goodbye for now and thank you. I can't help feeling that I will meet him again in some form or other.

Whilst on the subject of animals, I would like to add the experience of losing my beloved Chihuahua Totty. John and I had known she was near her death; she was fifteen years old and had become very weak. She died in bed with both of us; we had been wakened by her coughing and we knew it was the end. Suddenly we heard her death rattle and then she went limp. It was about 3.30 in the morning and the room was in darkness, but at that moment the room seemed to light up and we could actually feel her spirit rise up from us. The most amazing thing was that as she left we heard the song of a bird. She had been so important in my work and had spent most of her life in my consulting room. I always felt her power was there to help. I know she was back in the light and her death was a most moving spiritual experience but the pain of losing her was so severe that I could not speak to anyone for over a week. So even though my beliefs are so strong and I knew she was in a beautiful place, the pain I felt was like a physical pain in my heart that stayed for a very long time. Even writing this small piece now has brought forward floods of tears. I'm sure when my turn finally comes to go to the light she will be among the first to greet me.

Since writing this piece, in one of my communications with Ev, he told me that Totty is with him. This I felt sure about anyway, as she was the beloved pet of both of us in marriage; in fact, she was like our baby.

CHAPTER TEN

❖

The Positive Effects of Regression

I n this final chapter I'd like to recap on some of the things I have written up to now. I have tried to give a rounded picture of the different aspects of regression: recurring likes and dislikes; fears, phobias and recurring dreams; how the same people are brought back to carry on where they left off together in a prior existence so that love grows over many lifetimes; meeting our pets again in a different form; changing from male and female to complete our incarnations. I also feel that this whole book shows that there is no such thing as death, only an end to each life.

In fact, since beginning my journeys into the past and seeing many of my earlier incarnations set out before me I have discovered that many of my friends, too numerous to name, have all been with me before. The positive aspect of seeing these lives is to make me understand more fully each friend or relative's part in my present life. How many of the people in your own lives do you feel you have known before? I have even met people who have declared that on looking into the eyes of their baby for the first time they felt that they already knew each other, that the child was an old soul.

I feel it is sad that reincarnation is not taken as a natural thing. Like many other natural and instinctive wisdoms, we seem to have lost so much of our knowledge from the past. We seem to think that we have progressed through the ages. I know we have scientifically, but I feel that this is not so spiritually; we may even have lost more than we have gained.

Mind you, if the tales of lives in Atlantis are to be believed, then even scientifically we have not progressed! I have heard many people state that they have been told that they had a life in Atlantis but have never in all my regressions come across my kind of proof of it. I must say, though, that I have heard of the use of crystals in Atlantis on many occasions, and I do think we have not yet put crystal power to full use. We have probably only scratched the surface of its potential.

The conclusion and also consolation I draw from all this is that there is a general movement to restore the importance of some of the intuitive knowledge that at one time was common to us. In my quest to support this movement, I have often been attacked by members of religious movements, and I find this sad because it indicates a closed-mindedness, and a forgetfulness of some of their own teachings. As an example I would like to quote from Mary Harrison's book *Life before Birth* in which she draws our attention to the section of the Bible where it is suggested that John the Baptist had come in the spirit of Elijah; a passage that suggests to me that John was the reincarnation of Elijah. It also appears that at the time of the ministry of Jesus on earth, the idea of reincarnation must have been an accepted one, even amongst his disciples, because when Jesus asked them who they thought he was they gave various answers, all indicating that the idea of a soul of a dead person coming back to earth in a different physical body was not foreign or strange to them. From their response to him, it is clear that a belief in reincarnation must have been an everyday part of their lives. As we all know, the Bible has been changed and tampered with many times throughout the ages, often by people who wished to use the words of this book for their own power over their congregations. I wonder when these kinds of references to past lives were dropped and for what reason?

I hope my book shows how helpful this knowledge of one's past can be. Life is always hard – it is not meant to be easy – but it can be blissful if looked at truthfully and with faith. My own life is a good example of this. I understand my weaknesses and allow for them. I know I froze to death in China and have always suffered from the cold. I have seen a life as a white African living in a tree house and caring for animals, another love in this life. I have seen four lives where I used the power of healing: in an Inca life as a trance temple girl, something I have used again in this time; as a shaman in the Indian life; and twice as a nun, once in France and then in Spain. I was also shown, and have in this life, been heavily connected to and influenced by a life I had as a French dandy, a homosexual. I saw myself bewigged, powdered and beauty-spotted in the French court about the time Elton was strutting his stuff; I was even shown my lover, who was a soldier. Later he was shown to me in a reincarnation as one of my dearest lady friends, a lady called Vera, in my present life. In fact, this particular friend became very ill about twenty years ago and I took her to a sitting with a person I then worked with who had much to do with my development as a healer, and was told that Vera was soon to work with me. I instantly took that to mean that she would recover. However, she died not long afterwards, but has worked with me from the other side of life for years in the most amazing, miraculous way. Obviously the power of our love remained strong enough to make such an astonishing link from the other side, even though this love grew in a homosexual way.

How can anyone judge lovers? I was reminded of this life only recently in a communication with my ex- and late husband Kenny when it was pointed out that I had understood him and his needs this time because I too had been on that same route. The fact that I had experienced homosexual love and that I had been his mother in two past lives, made me the ideal partner for his early development in this last life of his. Since Kenny died I have had many communications with him and so have lots of his other loved ones, but the most interesting aspect of his death is that many of my clients – when low and needy and praying for help from me – have seen and in some cases even felt the touch of him. As he said in his very first communication to me, he is intended to work alongside and help me in this life, and up to now he has been proved right. We did have a very strong bond and, like Vera, in spirit I feel we have the power of love that makes the link from the other side.

When I get low, as is only natural in the physical, I can always gain help and strength from them and many others. In fact, I have many helpers (as do lots of other workers). When Billy Fury died he came through to me in the presence of Kenny and John and two other friends and seemed to take over the room. I had at that time published the first autobiography of my life and was about to embark on a media tour to promote it. The first booking was in Birmingham at Radio BRMB, it was a show called 'Profile' hosted by the now programme director Mike Owen. Mike didn't believe in any of the stuff I was involved in. The show was to be taped and put out on air later. Mike covered my life briefly and after each section played a record of my choice. Everything went well until we began to talk about Billy and then I felt him overshadow me. I remember thinking that he was coming on tour with me. As Mike chatted about him I felt him leave me and take Mike over. It was really dramatic: we had to stop the tape and I gave Mike healing, during which he nearly fell asleep. We tried again. Once more, in came Billy and I had to help Mike again. Mike really did get proof as he told me he actually saw Billy as he approached him. The live news broadcast in the adjoining studio actually broke down at the same time too! Mike has since changed his whole view on the spiritual and has even given after-dinner speeches on the subject. So, you see how all my loved ones seem to work alongside me in this life.

That also bears out my theory that when we elect to come

to the earth-plane to work out our karmic path, all our loved ones become part of our auras and choose their most suitable role to help, depending on their past experience with us. It is a very common thing to hear people say that they feel the help of loved ones in spirit, and I have heard many stories of people actually seeing their loved ones shortly after their passing either with the naked eye or, more commonly, in vivid dreams.

Another life I was shown was as a Japanese girl working in the paddy fields. Myself and other girl workers were knee-deep in water, picking the rice. On the adjoining bank was a male overseer, who appeared to be drinking something like sake. There was much laughter and we girls seemed to be making him the butt of many jokes, which he took light-heartedly. He then drove us in a rough, horse-driven cart back to our villages, but as we approached the sky was bright red and I actually felt the heat of our villages burning. We arrived to find Samurai warriors had torched our homes and killed all our families and as I ran through the street towards my home a soldier galloped up to me and sliced off the top of my head. At the regression, I did not think I was dead and the therapist had to make me look at my mutilated body on the ground.

This oriental life seems to have had a great influence on my present life as I have many Eastern artefacts and John and I collect ceramic china figures. I also have a large Japanese doll in full bridal outfit that I am besotted with and every time I have moved homes I never pack her but always carry her in my car with me, along with a crystal nun that I also treasure. I can't help feeling that the bridal doll is what I would have been looking forward to dressing like in my Japanese incarnation had it not been curtailed so early!

I often ask my clients after a series of regressions to look around their homes and identify the many hangovers from earlier tastes; it provides many clues to our past history. John and I are great fans of the television show *Time Team*. Viewers write in about sites that they feel would be historically interesting, and the archaeologists on the team set about to explore the sites. They collect tiny pieces of broken pottery and other things from the ground and then piece together the history of the site and come up with interesting, often quite amazing information about the lifestyle and habits of the people who lived there hundreds of years ago. Also interesting is that many of the ancient wall and floor tiling and decorations they unearth are almost identical to some of today's designs. Could new designs draw on the soul memory, in the same way that comedians say that all jokes are derived from the one original joke? I think so. The work of these archaeologists, I feel, is very much like my work, as I have to do detective work in people's psyches to piece together information about their pasts. I feel some of my findings are equally important, as many different feelings, as well as artefacts, have been trapped in the grounds of time, and my job is slowly to clear away the earth above them and set them free.

I remember one time being taken to an ancient Native American monument in Arizona called Montezuma's Castle. I was with Kenny and we were looking forward to our visit there as all the dug-out caves in the cliffs have been preserved extremely well. I had only just stepped inside the site when I was overtaken by extreme, overwhelming sadness and could not stop crying. Kenny had to take me back to our hotel as I was devastated. We never even got to explore the castle. We could find nothing in the guide books to explain why the past residents of the site had disappeared; nothing about their end was recorded. I feel they all died at that spot and the feeling of sadness and tragedy remains trapped in the earth. In fact, there have been many places that I feel I could never visit. I have a psychic friend who, I felt, was foolish to visit a German prisoner of war camp and she took ages to shake off the overwhelming feeling that she collected there. I have been told that there are never any birds at these sites, nor any flowers, yet another proof of the pain that can become trapped there. Surely most of those tragic victims that have re-incarnated would benefit from regression.

In the same way, many homes that have seen tragedy would benefit from clearance, as it is a very common thing for me to see a client who is experiencing a complete personality change after moving into a different home. I generally find that there has been a tragedy in the place which is overshadowing them, often throwing them into extreme depression and even suicidal moods.

Finally, I have as a guide a very wise and old Chinese man and I am amazed that I have never been shown a life that connects with him. I feel, because he came to me later in my development, that this life is yet to be shown to me at the right time. I have, over the years, been given many paintings and drawings of his likeness and most of the Chinese ceramics of men I have look very like him. In a couple of these paintings there is a tiny canary in his wide sleeve. I was told that this bird was my late-lamented Chihuahua, Totty, the same little dog that opened up my healing power. Strangely enough, before I knew these things – when she was a tiny puppy – she used to squeal when she got excited and all my friends used to say she sounded just like a bird. This bird sound left her as she grew up, rather like the children who are born with past-life memory lose their recall as they grow up. My faithful Chinaman's name is Ling Foo, and even though I do not yet know when or what our powerful connection is, I have put my faith in him for many years now. I would like to dedicate this book to him and all my other helpers on the other side.

And to conclude, I have asked a few of my clients to say – in their own words – what regression has done for them, so that we can demonstrate from experience the way it works. Here is the first account.

'For quite a few years I had back pain that seemed to stem from my stomach. I had this pain every so often; sometimes it was so bad that I had to go on all fours to try to stop it. The pain continued after I had my two children. Eventually it became more and more frequent and I suppose, like anyone who has had pain for years, you sort of accept it. I had been to doctors who couldn't find anything wrong and I just thought that I would have to live with it. But the pain was so frequent that it was interfering with my everyday life and sapping my energy. I couldn't lift my children or bend to pick up anything off the floor, and running was impossible. I then met Lee and booked an appointment with her for a regression, not knowing what to expect.

'Regression feels like you are describing your own home movie. Although you see a person who doesn't look anything like you, you just know that it is you. I was with a group of Native Americans looking down on a group of people with wagons and it looked as if they were camping for the night. Before I knew it, I was part of a fight. There was screaming, shouting, arrows and what looked like hatchets flying everywhere and I was very frightened. Then I was shot in the back. The pain was unbelievable – I could feel it in my stomach –it was exactly the same pain I had suffered for the last five years.

'I can honestly say that from that day I have never had that pain again. It was cleared completely in the regression. I don't know how it works, all I know is that it definitely worked for me. If it hadn't been for Lee, I would have had that pain for the rest of my life. I thank Lee for everything.'

This next regression shows how fears and phobias can be overcome, and how regression can give you more insight into your own character in this life, thereby enabling you to cope better.

'I've been regressed by Lee on two occasions. At the time of my first visit to her in London I was still using drugs and alcohol. I was apprehensive about the regression and decided to have a little cocaine beforehand. I arrived at her home only to find that she had had to go out on an emergency and therefore couldn't see me that day. I felt that it was meant that I should not have gone to her drugged so on my second visit I decided to go without any assistance.

'I saw very clearly myself in a house probably in the last century. Lee helped me through the house, down a staircase into a large room with a man leaning against the fireplace. I didn't feel at all at ease with this person; in fact, very uncomfortable. We moved on and I found myself standing beside a grave, but I suddenly realised that I wasn't by the side of it, but in it. I had been shot by the person by the fireplace because of a relationship. Lee asked me to look up for the light, which I did. I saw an incredibly bright light which I seemed to float up to. I still remember how great I felt, like I had found something. During the session I saw many little twinkling lights in the room as well as lights around the door. Lee explained that there were spirit lights in the room and that they were helping me.

'I was regressed again by Lee about a year later, and the thing I realised about both regressions was that in both lives I had been a very jealous person. In the first life I had been shot by the person I had seen by the fireplace because of a relationship, and in the second life I had been the murderer in a similar situation. For this crime I saw myself being hanged and my body taken away on a cart. Without doubt, I realise that both these regressions have helped me see my failings in relationships I have had, and helped me to cope with them. I gave up drugs and alcohol five years ago, but am now able to have a few drinks now and then without any problem. This I know I could not have done without the help of Lee.'

This next account also testifies to the value of regression when coping with phobias.

'Before my first regression, I had a phobia about things above my head; I was convinced they were going to fall on my head so I would always find myself avoiding walking underneath overhanging objects. During the regression, I saw myself as a lumberjack. A tree fell over and I died as a result. After the regression, my phobia disappeared.

'I also had a phobia about sharp knives or razor blades. I was convinced that I would injure myself whenever I came into contact with them. This became much worse when I was a teenager, and I reached the stage where I couldn't even bring myself to look at a sharp implement. Over the past few years I began to experience a slashing sensation around my face, which became gradually stronger and prompted me to have a second regression.

'I saw myself as a middle-aged, quite wealthy Japanese woman. One day some intruders came to the house and I helped my husband and son to escape, but as a result I was caught, then taken away and executed, even though it was my husband they were seeking. I was killed by decapitation, but it took several attempts before they were successful, and I feel this explains my fear of sharp knives. After the regression, I felt a lot better. The slashing sensation lessened and has now disappeared completely.'

Regression is a very spiritual experience, as this next testimony shows.

'I sought out Lee for regression at a very low point in my life. My marriage was over, I feared losing my two sons and my career was in the doldrums. The overall feeling was one of failure. I felt mentally and spiritually "blocked". I hoped that regression would help me on a deeper level.

'I saw myself sitting on the side of a Tuscan square. It was a hot, dusty day and shafts of sunlight cut across my table. The publican, who knew me well, served me something simple and offered words of comfort and encouragement. I was very nervous and tense. I sensed that this was a day that could change my life. Looking down, I could see a pair of rusty-coloured hose, short, dusty boots and a simple brown doublet.

'At last a young man of my age came out of a building on the opposite side of the square and headed towards me. I got up, leaving the food I was too nervous to touch, and walked across to the same building. I climbed a wooden spiral staircase. By the time I reached the door on the landing, I knew that I was to meet my tutor and that behind the door lay the key to my future.

'The details of the meeting are obscure but by the time I returned to the square, I was elated. I had passed some form of assessment, had become a scholar and was off to Rome to study with the best in the world. I was shown a tearful leave-taking with my parents and brother.

'Immediately after the regression, I remember a sense of anti-climax. This could not be the miracle I had hoped for; it didn't seem relevant. The experience itself had been wonderful, the memories clear, precise and in marvellous Technicolor, but how was it going to lift me in the here and now?

'Over the following weeks, the vivid visual side of the regression began to fade and I was left with the memory of the feelings as if they were new. The most powerful one was the intense elation of my success. In the end, this became the dominant feature of the regression – I had "remembered" success. Gradually this memory began to have a positive effect on my life: the negativity lifted and I felt "unblocked". The conviction that I was a failure dispersed and my mind was once again open to the positive. I have had other regressions, but this one and the one that released me from a cycle of identical nightmares are probably the most powerful and important to me.'

Events in this life can trigger a past-life memory to be brought forward. Understanding that memory can help us cope with this life. Here is a another example.

'I went to see Lee because I was constantly getting the smell of burnt rubber. For quite a long time I had ignored it, thinking it was my imagination. Then I started to recall a dream in which people were burning to death.

'I had no idea what to expect of a regression. But when we sat I pictured myself as a young girl of about twelve years of age standing on a river bank. I had come from a fairly wealthy family and it had been while I was walking by the river that my home and family had been deliberately set on fire. This left me an orphan and, like many destitute young girls of that time, I was put in a brothel and my purpose in life was reduced to being an object for the entertainment of men. The worst part of it was that I was kept in a very damp cellar room and was only brought out when it was my time to entertain a man. Then I was bathed and dressed very well, just to be abused by these so-called gentlemen who always reeked of alcohol.

'Lee guided me through this life until I reached the age of forty and was no longer attractive enough to be considered useful. I spent the rest of my days in my cellar room with no self-respect and completely broken.

'The link to my present life which Lee thought had brought this memory forward was that I had just emerged from a thirty-year marriage with very little self-esteem. It appears I had repeated that old pattern of being servile to a man and now have to deal with it. Having the regression helped me see why I felt so strongly about certain things that were happening to me and helped me to deal with them. It is not simple, but I have become so much stronger because of this.'

Understanding relationships – often destructive ones – can be helped by regression, as can finding our own motives and our own ways in this life. Listen to this testimony.

'I had embarked on a relationship that had started out in instant attraction, then deteriorated into lies and games and become very destructive, even though I still loved this person. I was so puzzled by this that when a friend recommended Lee I made an appointment with her immediately for a regression.

'I went back to a life in Eastern Europe at the beginning of the Second World War. I was a teenage girl with a younger brother whom I adored – we were devoted to each other. After seeing around the house we lived in I was brought to a point where I had just entered my brother's room. I went to gently shake and kiss him awake when a bomb dropped and we were all killed. I was left feeling guilty about my brother as he was younger and more vulnerable than I and I felt I should have protected him.

'Lee told me to take my brother's hand and ascend into the light. This was a new experience for me as I knew nothing of when we die. I went into a bright, white light, an experience that made me feel alive and not afraid of dying. In the light, Lee asked me if there was anyone to greet us and I told her of a man with sky blue eyes who greeted us with arms outstretched. Lee told me he was one of my helpers.

'Lee then brought me back to the room in Hammersmith and I knew all my questions about things I couldn't understand had fallen into place and I had no need to be afraid any more. We also realised that the man with whom I was having the relationship had been my brother in that past life, hence my continuing love for him.

'I returned to Lee later because for a long time I had had an overwhelming desire to work with adults who had been abused as children, especially those who had been sexually abused by their mothers. This made me look very closely at myself and started me questioning whether I too had been abused.

'In this second regression, Lee took me back into my present life to the day I was born in a London hospital at the end of the War and then through most of my life. I looked at my feelings of rejection and loneliness when my mother had died and I had been put into a boarding school at the tender age of seven, and so on through my rape at sixteen and right up to the present day. There was no childhood abuse apart from the rape. Lee told me that my mother had been very much present through the reliving of the life and was going to guide me on my new spiritual path. I felt her love and have been helped by this new feeling.'

And here is one final comment on how regression can change people's lives for the better.

'I first met Lee socially over twenty years ago and that chance meeting was to change my life completely. She became my counsellor and confidante and began the process of helping me unravel a complex and traumatic life to date. Whilst in counsel with her, she would know instinctively whether my problem was past or present.

'My first regression took me back to my childhood in this present life. I was about two years old and desperately trying to open a door, but I could not reach the handle. I was in a terrible state of panic and crying hysterically. This caused me so much distress that Lee brought me back to the present.

'Later, while visiting my mother and looking through the family album, there was a photo of the same door I had seen in this regression. The picture was taken in Germany when I was a baby. I told my mother of my experience and she was able to tell me exactly what had happened.

'We were in an army house and the officers were provided with domestic help. Ours was a large, angry woman by the name of Helga. Mum had gone shopping and left us with Helga. She was fanatically clean so promptly put us children in the garden. I had been toilet-trained by the age of eighteen months, so when I realised I needed the toilet I tried to get back into the house. My banging on the door was not heard and I eventually wet my pants. Helga at that point opened the door and was very angry with me. She stripped off my clothes and placed me screaming in my cot where I remained until my mother returned.

'I had suffered all my life up to the regression with a weak bladder and cystitis plagued me constantly. After the regression I have had no problems whatsoever with urinary problems of any kind.

'My next regression took me back before Victorian times. I was a filthy little boy with holes in my shoes and rags for clothes. My death came at the age of seven, trapped whilst cleaning a chimney. It took a long time to die and I was in absolute despair. I remember vividly seeing myself picking my nose, which seemed to give me some comfort while I was waiting to die.

'Lee took me from the chimney into a wonderful white light where all pain disappeared. Later I realised that the blackness that surrounded me in the chimney was exactly like the feelings of blackness that had been coming over me for many years, having the effect of deep depressions which even resulted in two nervous breakdowns. After that, many of the black clouds left me.

'On a lighter note, I had always picked my nose as a child; a bad habit that my parents had tried to cure me of. It was a habit I thought I had developed in this life; but I now know it was stored in my memory and every time I was stressed I would resort to a finger in the nose.

'The most important of my regressions was so personal that I could not repeat it in print because it would be too distressing for the person involved. When I told Lee of some of the experiences I was having, she understood immediately, and with gentle guidance I was taken into the life and all was revealed to me – it was unspeakable horror! The person who caused this horror for me in that lifetime had become a very important part of my present life. The link is now severed, but it was severed with love, as after the regression I understood so much about the mixed feelings I had while our lives were linked. The true separation of our paths only came for me when I realised that I had forgiven them.

'I have since had many regressions with Lee and each time I have been shown something that had to be cleared. Somehow it has all gone into making me realise the meaning of my lives and my purpose. So thanks to Lee's guidance and development, I am now a registered healer and counsellor, and with this great love I feel for my fellow human beings I can be of help to others who cross my path.

'My love and gratitude to Lee for being paced on my path cannot be expressed with words; there are none big enough. Thank you, Lee.'

It is very difficult to draw conclusions and to summarise the experiences that people have when they undergo regression, as it seems that regression is totally personal and unique.

The regressions I have detailed in this book have taken place over a period of about six years. Although I knew that I would eventually write down the experiences in a book, I did not have a precise form in which I intended to relate the experiences. That structure came at a later stage. So I approached the research in a similar way to my normal regression work.

In some fundamental ways, however, it was very different. In my normal regression work, clients come to me of their own accord. In most cases, they already believe in reincarnation, in the movement of the soul through a series of lifetimes. For this book, I approached the celebrities and asked whether they would undergo regression; quite a different starting point. This has meant that they did not necessarily share my beliefs about regression; some were open-minded, others more than a little doubtful. Because of the circumstances, all approached me with a more sceptical and cautious mind than I would usually expect, not least because they knew their memories were going to end up in print.

Over many years of spiritual counselling and healing, I have learned to remove my mind, or my conscious thinking processes, from what I am doing; to stand aside and not to pass judgement. At the end of the regressions, my conscious mind returns at the same time as the client's mind 'comes round' and they emerge from the meditative state in which they have experienced their soul memories. As we reach this point, I am continually amazed at the intensity I can see in the other person's face. Some are in awe at the strength of feeling; some in shock or surprise; some simply crying with emotion.

It is my belief that somehow during these experiences, people are put in touch with their inner selves, even their souls – that part of us which is truly eternal. This contact, in itself, brings about healing. The result of the experience of regression and this contact with the soul is that the person frequently begins to pursue a more spiritual path, a path which I believe is the only way to fulfilment. Never be afraid to follow your instincts, for they come from your soul.

Our memories, like true love, never die. All the positive effects of our past still exist and bring new dimensions to our present. Take, for example, my past life as the nun, Sister Theresa. In my present life, I do not belong to a recognised Church. But the Catholic soul memory of Sister Theresa has left me with many strong emotional feelings aroused by Catholic images. These images stir me inside in a deeply emotional way, and I feel a reverence for that way of life. And so it is with all my other soul memories. I find that they are the essential me, the inner self that so many of us seek. I found this inner self with the help of regression.

Index